D0783656

THE NATION'S FAVOURITE POEMS

— ✦ —

FOREWORD BY

GRIFF RHYS JONES

Published by
BBC Worldwide Limited,
Woodlands,
80 Wood Lane,
London W12 OTT
First published 1996
Reprinted 1996 (6 times)
1997 (11 times)
1998 (4 times)
First published in hardback 1998

ISBN 0 563 38782 3 (paperback)
ISBN 0 563 38487 5 (hardback)

Set in 10/13 Stempel Garamond
Printed in Great Britain by Martins the Printers Ltd, Berwick-upon-Tweed
Bound in Great Britain by Hunter and Foulis Ltd, Edinburgh
Cover printed by Belmont Press, Northampton.
Jacket printed by Lawrence Allen Ltd, Weston-super-Mare.

CONTENTS

— ◇ —

FOREWORD BY GRIFF RHYS JONES

— ❖ —

To coincide with National Poetry Day 1995, the nation's favourite book programme, *The Bookworm*, conducted a poll to discover the nation's favourite poem. What we expected, I do not know; possibly that no one who watched television would have the slightest interest in poetry, that dirty limericks would dominate, that Shakespeare or Wordsworth would romp home. In the end, twelve thousand votes were posted and, furthermore, there soon emerged a clear and unassailable winner: Rudyard Kiplings's 'If'. At the final count it got twice as many votes as the runner up.

'If' was written at 'Batemans' in Burwash, Sussex, and published in 1910 in *Rewards and Fairies*. The Kaiser had a copy on his desk, it was Marie Stopes' favourite, and it was translated into Italian by Antonio Gramsci, the leader of the Italian Communist party in the 1930s. 'Jingoistic Rubbish' one paper called it when it won, but, clearly its sinuous rhythm gets a hold on people who like to get things done. Nonetheless, if you can't keep your head with 'If', there are another ninety-nine poems to enjoy here.

It quickly becomes clear anyway that the overall mood of the poll is hardly one of war-mongering tub thumpery. 'The Daffodils', 'To Autumn', 'The Lake Isle of Innisfree', 'Ode to a Nightingale', 'I Remember': the majority of the poems here have a wistful, yearning note. There is plenty of dissonance to give some edge to the collection, from Wilfred Owen, Marvell, Eliot and Stevie Smith amongst others, and there are a few nursery poems and comical ballads to lighten things up. (Children came out in strong support of Allan Ahlberg's wonderful. 'Please Mrs Butler'.) Some unexpected and unfamiliar poems also crop up, 'Emmonsail's Heath in Winter', for example, is a new John Clare to me; but taken together, the nation's preferred one hundred poems seem a reasonably balanced and representative selection of the best of English verse.

You may be surprised that Walter de la Mare came in ahead of Shakespeare. I was. But we found in the case of the greatest poets, that the popularity of all their poetry tended to split their vote. Wordsworth's support, for example, was divided between Westminster Bridge and the Lake District. Had we been judging on the basis solely of favourite poet then Keats, W.B. Yeats and W.H. Auden would have been the top three.

There were few votes for living poets, despite the current 'poetry boom'. Jenny Joseph was the most popular. Her poem 'Warning', about growing old disgracefully came in at number 22. Most of the living poets were women, but the dead poets were predominantly male.

Perhaps it was a matter for gratitude that there weren't many candidates from the obscure Independant Monster Raving Loony Versifiers party. The solitary poem with a solitary vote, possibly from its solitary author, was a fairly rare occurrence, voting was admirably free of faction and party politics and some of the more obscure entries, taken down by the over-stretched telephonists, turned out on closer inspection to be more familiar than first thought. 'He Who Author' was probably 'Hiawatha', 'Ozzy Mandias' was not, in fact, an ode to an Australian bricklayer, and 'Allergy in a Country Churchyard' was not the first draft of Noel Coward's *Hay Fever*.

A cynic might be tempted to claim that people voted for what they could remember; cherishing whatever they were forced to cherish at school, but if this is merely a collection of 'O' Level standard English Primer gems, then we ought to be grateful to the nation's English masters. Personally, I find fragments of what I stuffed in at fourth form level spinning up, unbidden, in solitary moments and when it does it's oddly potent. Useful too. I worked as a handbag checker on the back door of the Hilton in 1976, and when the music stopped at 2.30a.m. there was nothing to do on a twelve hour night shift except trace the pattern on the carpet and dig about inside my head for old, half-remembered verse. I wished then I'd been forced to learn more poems at school, and I still do.

Outside the competition, the unexpected poetry success of the year from *The Bookworm*'s point of view was an anonymous work which featured in a piece on war poetry. 'Do not Stand at my Grave and Weep' was left in an envelope for his parents by Steven Cummins, a soldier killed on active service in Northern Ireland, to be opened in the event of his death. It provoked an extraordinary response. The requests for copies started coming in almost immediately and over the following weeks the demand rose to a total of some thirty thousand. It was thought at first that the soldier himself had written it, but this was not the case. Claims were made for nineteenth century magazines and the prayers of Navaho Indian priests, but in the end its origins remain a mystery. In some respects it became the nation's favourite poem by proxy and, despite it being outside the competition, we have decided to include it here, in prime, first past the post, poll position.

DO NOT STAND AT MY GRAVE AND WEEP

— ✧ —

Do not stand at my grave and weep;
I am not there. I do not sleep.
I am a thousand winds that blow.
I am the diamond glints on snow.
I am the sunlight on ripened grain.
I am the gentle autumn rain.
When you awaken in the morning's hush
I am the swift uplifting rush
Of quiet birds in circled flight.
I am the soft stars that shine at night.
Do not stand at my grave and cry;
I am not there. I did not die.

RUDYARD KIPLING 1865–1936
_____

IF –

'Brother Square-Toes' – *Rewards and Fairies*

If you can keep your head when all about you
    Are losing theirs and blaming it on you,
If you can trust yourself when all men doubt you,
    But make allowance for their doubting too;
If you can wait and not be tired by waiting,
    Or being lied about, don't deal in lies,
Or being hated, don't give way to hating,
    And yet don't look too good, nor talk too wise:

If you can dream – and not make dreams your master;
    If you can think – and not make thoughts your aim;
If you can meet with Triumph and Disaster
    And treat those two impostors just the same;
If you can bear to hear the truth you've spoken
    Twisted by knaves to make a trap for fools,
Or watch the things you gave your life to, broken,
    And stoop and build 'em up with worn-out tools:

If you can make one heap of all your winnings
    And risk it on one turn of pitch-and-toss,
And lose, and start again at your beginnings
    And never breathe a word about your loss;
If you can force your heart and nerve and sinew
    To serve your turn long after they are gone,
And so hold on when there is nothing in you
    Except the Will which says to them: 'Hold on!'

If you can talk with crowds and keep your virtue,
    Or walk with Kings – nor lose the common touch,
If neither foes nor loving friends can hurt you,
    If all men count with you, but none too much;
If you can fill the unforgiving minute
    With sixty seconds' worth of distance run,
Yours is the Earth and everything that's in it,
    And – which is more – you'll be a Man, my son!

ALFRED, LORD TENNYSON 1809–92

THE LADY OF SHALOTT

PART I

On either side the river lie
Long fields of barley and of rye,
That clothe the wold and meet the sky;
And thro' the field the road runs by
      To many-tower'd Camelot;
And up and down the people go,
Gazing where the lilies blow
Round an island there below,
      The island of Shalott.

Willows whiten, aspens quiver,
Little breezes dusk and shiver
Thro' the wave that runs for ever
By the island in the river
      Flowing down to Camelot.
Four grey walls, and four grey towers,
Overlook a space of flowers,
And the silent isle imbowers
      The Lady of Shalott.

By the margin, willow-veil'd,
Slide the heavy barges trail'd
By slow horses; and unhail'd
The shallop flitteth silken-sail'd
      Skimming down to Camelot:
But who hath seen her wave her hand?
Or at the casement seen her stand?
Or is she known in all the land,
      The Lady of Shalott?

Only reapers, reaping early
In among the bearded barley,
Hear a song that echoes cheerly
From the river winding clearly,
      Down to tower'd Camelot:

And by the moon the reaper weary,
Piling sheaves in uplands airy,
Listening, whispers ''Tis the fairy
        Lady of Shalott.'

PART II

There she weaves by night and day
A magic web with colours gay.
She has heard a whisper say,
A curse is on her if she stay
        To look down to Camelot.
She knows not what the curse may be,
And so she weaveth steadily,
And little other care hath she,
        The Lady of Shalott.

And moving thro' a mirror clear
That hangs before her all the year,
Shadows of the world appear.
There she sees the highway near
        Winding down to Camelot:
There the river eddy whirls,
And there the surly village-churls,
And the red cloaks of market girls,
        Pass onward from Shalott.

Sometimes a troop of damsels glad,
An abbot on an ambling pad,
Sometimes a curly shepherd-lad,
Or long-hair'd page in crimson clad,
        Goes by to tower'd Camelot;
And sometimes thro' the mirror blue
The knights come riding two and two:
She hath no loyal knight and true,
        The Lady of Shalott.

But in her web she still delights
To weave the mirror's magic sights,
For often thro' the silent nights
A funeral, with plumes and lights,
      And music, went to Camelot:
Or when the moon was overhead,
Came two young lovers lately wed;
'I am half sick of shadows,' said
      The Lady of Shalott.

PART III

A bow-shot from her bower-eaves,
He rode between the barley-sheaves,
The sun came dazzling thro' the leaves,
And flamed upon the brazen greaves
      Of bold Sir Lancelot.
A red-cross knight for ever kneel'd
To a lady in his shield,
That sparkled on the yellow field,
      Beside remote Shalott.

The gemmy bridle glitter'd free,
Like to some branch of stars we see
Hung in the golden Galaxy.
The bridle bells rang merrily
      As he rode down to Camelot:
And from his blazon'd baldric slung
A mighty silver bugle hung,
And as he rode his armour rung,
      Beside remote Shalott.

All in the blue unclouded weather
Thick-jewell'd shone the saddle-leather,
The helmet and the helmet-feather
Burn'd like one burning flame together,
      As he rode down to Camelot.
As often thro' the purple night,
Below the starry clusters bright,
Some bearded meteor, trailing light,
      Moves over still Shalott.

His broad clear brow in sunlight glow'd;
On burnish'd hooves his war-horse trode;
From underneath his helmet flow'd
His coal-black curls as on he rode,
　　As he rode down to Camelot.
From the bank and from the river
He flash'd into the crystal mirror,
'Tirra lirra,' by the river
　　Sang Sir Lancelot.

She left the web, she left the loom,
She made three paces thro' the room,
She saw the water-lily bloom,
She saw the helmet and the plume,
　　She look'd down to Camelot.
Out flew the web and floated wide;
The mirror crack'd from side to side;
'The curse is come upon me,' cried
　　The Lady of Shalott.

PART IV
In the stormy east-wind straining,
The pale yellow woods were waning,
The broad stream in his banks complaining,
Heavily the low sky raining
　　Over tower'd Camelot;
Down she came and found a boat
Beneath a willow left afloat,
And round about the prow she wrote
　　The Lady of Shalott.

And down the river's dim expanse –
Like some bold seer in a trance,
Seeing all his own mischance –
With a glassy countenance
　　Did she look to Camelot.
And at the closing of the day
She loosed the chain, and down she lay;
The broad stream bore her far away,
　　The Lady of Shalott.

Lying, robed in snowy white
That loosely flew to left and right –
The leaves upon her falling light –
Thro' the noises of the night
       She floated down to Camelot:
And as the boat-head wound along
The willowy hills and fields among,
They heard her singing her last song.
       The Lady of Shalott.

Heard a carol, mournful, holy,
Chanted loudly, chanted lowly,
Till her blood was frozen slowly,
And her eyes were darken'd wholly,
       Turn'd to tower'd Camelot.
For ere she reach'd upon the tide
The first house by the water-side,
Singing in her song she died
       The Lady of Shalott.

Under tower and balcony,
By garden-wall and gallery,
A gleaming shape she floated by,
Dead-pale between the houses high,
       Silent into Camelot.
Out upon the wharfs they came,
Knight and burgher, lord and dame.
And round the prow they read her name,
       The Lady of Shalott.

Who is this? and what is here?
And in the lighted palace near
Died the sound of royal cheer;
And they cross'd themselves for fear,
       All the knights at Camelot:
But Lancelot mused a little space;
He said. 'She has a lovely face;
God in his mercy lend her grace.
       The Lady of Shalott.'

WALTER DE LA MARE 1873-1956

THE LISTENERS

'Is there anybody there?' said the Traveller,
    Knocking on the moonlit door;
And his horse in the silence champed the grasses
    Of the forest's ferny floor:
And a bird flew up out of the turret,
    Above the Traveller's head:
And he smote upon the door again a second time;
    'Is there anybody there?' he said.
But no one descended to the Traveller;
    No head from the leaf-fringed sill
Leaned over and looked into his grey eyes,
    Where he stood perplexed and still.
But only a host of phantom listeners
    That dwelt in the lone house then
Stood listening in the quiet of the moonlight
    To that voice from the world of men:
Stood thronging the faint moonbeams on the dark stair,
    That goes down to the empty hall,
Harkening in an air stirred and shaken
    By the lonely Traveller's call.
And he felt in his heart their strangeness,
    Their stillness answering his cry,
While his horse moved, cropping the dark turf,
    'Neath the starred and leafy sky;
For he suddenly smote on the door, even
    Louder, and lifted his head: –
'Tell them I came, and no one answered,
    That I kept my word,' he said.
Never the least stir made the listeners,
    Though every word he spake
Fell echoing through the shadowiness of the still house
    From the one man left awake:
Ay, they heard his foot upon the stirrup,
    And the sound of iron on stone,
And how the silence surged softly backward,
    When the plunging hoofs were gone.

4

STEVIE SMITH 1903–71

NOT WAVING BUT DROWNING

Nobody heard him, the dead man,
But still he lay moaning:
I was much further out than you thought
And not waving but drowning.

Poor chap, he always loved larking
And now he's dead
It must have been too cold for him his heart gave way,
They said.

Oh, no no no, it was too cold always
(Still the dead one lay moaning)
I was much too far out all my life
And not waving but drowning.

WILLIAM WORDSWORTH 1770–1850

THE DAFFODILS

I wander'd lonely as a cloud
That floats on high o'er vales and hills,
When all at once I saw a crowd,
A host of golden daffodils,
Beside the lake, beneath the trees
Fluttering and dancing in the breeze.

Continuous as the stars that shine
And twinkle on the milky way,
They stretch'd in never-ending line
Along the margin of a bay:
Ten thousand saw I at a glance
Tossing their heads in sprightly dance.

The waves beside them danced, but they
Out-did the sparkling waves in glee: –
A Poet could not but be gay
In such a jocund company!
I gazed – and gazed – but little thought
What wealth the show to me had brought.

For oft, when on my couch I lie
In vacant or in pensive mood,
They flash upon that inward eye
Which is the bliss of solitude;
And then my heart with pleasure fills
And dances with the daffodils.

JOHN KEATS 1795–1821

TO AUTUMN

Season of mists and mellow fruitfulness,
  Close bosom-friend of the maturing sun;
Conspiring with him how to load and bless
  With fruit the vines that round the thatch-eaves run;
To bend with apples the mossed cottage-trees,
  And fill all fruit with ripeness to the core;
    To swell the gourd, and plump the hazel shells
  With a sweet kernel; to set budding more,
And still more, later flowers for the bees,
Until they think warm days will never cease,
  For Summer has o'er-brimmed their clammy cells.

Who hath not seen thee oft amid thy store?
  Sometimes whoever seeks abroad may find
Thee sitting careless on a granary floor.
  Thy hair soft-lifted by the winnowing wind;
Or on a half-reaped furrow sound asleep.
  Drowsed with the fume of poppies, while thy hook
    Spares the next swath and all its twinèd flowers:
  And sometimes like a gleaner thou dost keep
Steady thy laden head across a brook;
Or by a cider-press, with patient look,
  Thou watchest the last oozings, hours by hours.

Where are the songs of Spring? Ay, where are they?
  Think not of them, thou hast thy music too –
While barrèd clouds bloom the soft-dying day,
  And touch the stubble-plains with rosy hue;
Then in a wailful choir the small gnats mourn
  Among the river sallows, borne aloft
    Or sinking as the light wind lives or dies;
  And full-grown lambs loud bleat from hilly bourn;
Hedge-crickets sing; and now with treble soft
The red-breast whistles from a garden croft;
  And gathering swallows twitter in the skies.

W.B. YEATS 1865–1939

THE LAKE ISLE OF INNISFREE

I will arise and go now, and go to Innisfree,
And a small cabin build there, of clay and wattles made:
Nine bean-rows will I have there, a hive for the honey-bee,
And live alone in the bee-loud glade.

And I shall have some peace there, for peace comes dropping slow,
Dropping from the veils of the morning to where the cricket sings;
There midnight's all a glimmer, and noon a purple glow,
And evening full of the linnet's wings.

I will arise and go now, for always night and day
I hear lake water lapping with low sounds by the shore;
While I stand on the roadway, or on the pavements grey,
I hear it in the deep heart's core.

WILFRED OWEN 1893–1918

DULCE ET DECORUM EST

Bent double, like old beggars under sacks,
Knock-kneed, coughing like hags, we cursed through sludge,
Till on the haunting flares we turned our backs
And towards our distant rest began to trudge.
Men marched asleep. Many had lost their boots
But limped on, blood-shod. All went lame; all blind;
Drunk with fatigue; deaf even to the hoots
Of tired, outstripped Five-Nines that dropped behind.

Gas! Gas! Quick, boys! – An ecstasy of fumbling,
Fitting the clumsy helmets just in time;
But someone still was yelling out and stumbling
And flound'ring like a man in fire or lime …
Dim, through the misty panes and thick green light,
As under a green sea, I saw him drowning.

In all my dreams, before my helpless sight,
He plunges at me, guttering, choking, drowning.

If in some smothering dreams you too could pace
Behind the wagon that we flung him in,
And watch the white eyes writhing in his face,
His hanging face, like a devil's sick of sin;
If you could hear, at every jolt, the blood
Come gargling from the froth-corrupted lungs,
Obscene as cancer, bitter as the cud
Of vile, incurable sores on innocent tongues, –
My friend, you would not tell with such high zest
To children ardent for some desperate glory,
The old Lie: Dulce et decorum est
Pro patria mori.

JOHN KEATS 1795-1821
———————————————
ODE TO A NIGHTINGALE

My heart aches, and a drowsy numbness pains
    My sense, as though of hemlock I had drunk,
Or emptied some dull opiate to the drains
    One minute past, and the Lethe-wards had sunk:
'Tis not through envy of thy happy lot,
    But being too happy in thy happiness, –
        That thou, light-wingèd Dryad of the trees,
            In some melodious plot
Of beechen green, and shadows numberless,
    Singest of summer in full-throated ease.

O for a draught of vintage! that hath been
    Cool'd a long age in the deep-delvèd earth,
Tasting of Flora and the country-green,
    Dance, and Provençal song, and sunburnt mirth.
O for a beaker full of the warm South,
    Full of the true, the blushful Hippocrene,
        With beaded bubbles winking at the brim
            And purple-stainèd mouth;
That I might drink, and leave the world unseen,
    And with thee fade away into the forest dim.

Fade far away, dissolve, and quite forget
    What thou among the leaves hast never known,
The weariness, the fever, and the fret
    Here, where men sit and hear each other groan;
Where palsy shakes a few, sad, last grey hairs,
    Where youth grows pale, and spectre-thin, and dies;
        Where but to think is to be full of sorrow
            And leaden-eyed despairs;
Where Beauty cannot keep her lustrous eyes,
    Or new Love pine at them beyond tomorrow.

Away! away! for I will fly to thee,
  Not charioted by Bacchus and his pards,
But on the viewless wings of Poesy,
  Though the dull brain perplexes and retards:
Already with thee! tender is the night,
  And haply the Queen-Moon is on her throne,
    Cluster'd around by all her starry Fays;
      But here there is no light
    Save what from heaven is with the breezes blown
      Through verdurous glooms and winding mossy ways.

I cannot see what flowers are at my feet,
  Nor what soft incense hangs upon the boughs,
But, in embalmèd darkness, guess each sweet
  Wherewith the seasonable month endows
The grass, the thicket, and the fruit-tree wild;
  White hawthorn, and the pastoral eglantine;
    Fast-fading violets cover'd up in leaves;
      And mid-May's eldest child
    The coming musk-rose, full of dewy wine,
      The murmurous haunt of flies on summer eves.

Darkling I listen; and for many a time
  I have been half in love with easeful Death,
Call'd him soft names in many a musèd rhyme,
  To take into the air my quiet breath;
Now more than ever seems it rich to die,
  To cease upon the midnight with no pain,
    While thou art pouring forth thy soul abroad
      In such an ecstasy!
    Still wouldst thou sing, and I have ears in vain –
      To thy high requiem become a sod.

Thou wast not born for death, immortal Bird!
No hungry generations tread thee down;
The voice I hear this passing night was heard
In ancient days by emperor and clown:
Perhaps the selfsame song that found a path
Through the sad heart of Ruth, when, sick for home,
She stood in tears amid the alien corn;
The same that oft-times hath
Charm'd magic casements, opening on the foam
Of perilous seas, in faery lands forlorn.

Forlorn! the very word is like a bell
To toll me back from thee to my sole self!
Adieu! the fancy cannot cheat so well
As she is famed to do, deceiving elf.
Adieu! adieu! thy plaintive anthem fades
Past the near meadows, over the still stream,
Up the hill-side; and now 'tis buried deep
In the next valley-glades:
Was it a vision, or a waking dream?
Fled is that music: – do I wake or sleep?

10

W.B. YEATS 1865-1939

HE WISHES FOR THE CLOTHS OF HEAVEN

Had I the heavens' embroidered cloths,
Enwrought with golden and silver light,
The blue and the dim and the dark cloths
Of night and light and the half-light,
I would spread the cloths under your feet:
But I, being poor, have only my dreams;
I have spread my dreams under your feet;
Tread softly because you tread on my dreams.

11

REMEMBER

Remember me when I am gone away,
  Gone far away into the silent land;
  When you can no more hold me by the hand,
Nor I half turn to go yet turning stay.
Remember me when no more day by day
  You tell me of our future that you planned:
  Only remember me; you understand
It will be late to counsel then or pray.
Yet if you should forget me for a while
  And afterwards remember, do not grieve:
  For if the darkness and corruption leave
A vestige of the thoughts that once I had,
Better by far you should forget and smile
  Than that you should remember and be sad.

12

THOMAS GRAY 1716–71

ELEGY WRITTEN IN A COUNTRY CHURCHYARD

The curfew tolls the knell of parting day,
  The lowing herd wind slowly o'er the lea,
The plowman homeward plods his weary way,
  And leaves the world to darkness and to me.

Now fades the glimmering landscape on the sight,
  And all the air a solemn stillness holds,
Save where the beetle wheels his droning flight,
  And drowsy tinklings lull the distant folds.

Save that from yonder ivy-mantled tower
  The moping owl does to the moon complain
Of such as, wandering near her secret bower,
  Molest her ancient solitary reign.

Beneath those rugged elms, that yew-tree's shade,
  Where heaves the turf in many a mouldering heap,
Each in his narrow cell for ever laid,
  The rude forefathers of the hamlet sleep.

The breezy call of incense-breathing morn,
  The swallow twittering from the straw-built shed,
The cock's shrill clarion, or the echoing horn,
  No more shall rouse them from their lowly bed.

For them no more the blazing hearth shall burn,
  Or busy housewife ply her evening care:
No children run to lisp their sire's return,
  Or climb his knee the envied kiss to share.

Oft did the harvest to their sickle yield,
  Their furrow of the stubborn glebe has broke:
How jocund did they drive their team afield!
  How bowed the woods beneath their sturdy stroke!

Let not ambition mock their useful toil,
  Their homely joys, and destiny obscure;
Nor grandeur hear with a disdainful smile
  The short and simple annals of the poor.

The boast of heraldry, the pomp of power,
And all that beauty, all that wealth e'er gave,
Awaits alike the inevitable hour.
The paths of glory lead but to the grave.

Nor you, ye proud, impute to these the fault,
If memory o'er their tomb no trophies raise,
Where through the long-drawn aisle and fretted vault
The pealing anthem swells the note of praise.

Can storied urn or animated bust
Back to its mansion call the fleeting breath?
Can honour's voice provoke the silent dust,
Or flattery soothe the dull cold ear of death?

Perhaps in this neglected spot is laid
Some heart once pregnant with celestial fire;
Hands, that the rod of empire might have swayed,
Or waked to extasy the living lyre.

But knowledge to their eyes her ample page
Rich with the spoils of time did ne'er unroll;
Chill penury repressed their noble rage,
And froze the genial current of the soul.

Full many a gem of purest ray serene,
The dark unfathomed caves of ocean bear;
Full many a flower is born to blush unseen,
And waste its sweetness on the desert air.

Some village-Hampden, that with dauntless breast
The little tyrant of his fields withstood,
Some mute inglorious Milton here may rest,
Some Cromwell guiltless of his country's blood.

The applause of listening senates to command.
The threats of pain and ruin to despise,
To scatter plenty o'er a smiling land,
And read their history in a nation's eyes,

Their lot forbad: nor circumscribed alone
Their growing virtues, but their crimes confined;
Forbad to wade through slaughter to a throne,
And shut the gates of mercy on mankind,

The struggling pangs of conscious truth to hide,
　To quench the blushes of ingenuous shame,
Or heap the shrine of luxury and pride
　With incense kindled at the Muse's flame.

Far from the madding crowd's ignoble strife,
　Their sober wishes never learned to stray;
Along the cool sequestered vale of life
　They kept the noiseless tenor of their way.

Yet even those bones from insult to protect
　Some frail memorial still erected nigh,
With uncouth rhymes and shapeless sculpture decked,
　Implores the passing tribute of a sigh.

Their name, their years, spelt by the unlettered Muse,
　The place of fame and elegy supply:
And many a holy text around she strews,
　That teach the rustic moralist to die.

For who, to dumb forgetfulness a prey,
　This pleasing anxious being e'er resigned,
Left the warm precincts of the cheerful day,
　Nor cast one longing lingering look behind?

On some fond breast the parting soul relies,
　Some pious drops the closing eye requires;
E'en from the tomb the voice of nature cries,
　E'en in our ashes live their wonted fires.

For thee, who mindful of the unhonoured dead,
　Dost in these lines their artless tale relate;
If chance, by lonely contemplation led,
　Some kindred spirit shall inquire thy fate –

Haply some hoary-headed swain may say,
　'Oft have we seen him at the peep of dawn
Brushing with hasty steps the dews away
　To meet the sun upon the upland lawn.

'There at the foot of yonder nodding beech,
　That wreathes its old fantastic roots so high,
His listless length at noontide would he stretch,
　And pore upon the brook that babbles by.

'Hard by yon wood, now smiling as in scorn,
  Muttering his wayward fancies he would rove,
Now drooping, woeful-wan, like one forlorn,
  Or crazed with care, or crossed in hopeless love.

'One morn I missed him on the customed hill,
  Along the heath, and near his favourite tree;
Another came; nor yet beside the rill,
  Nor up the lawn, nor at the wood was he:

'The next, with dirges due in sad array
  Slow through the church-way path we saw him borne.
Approach and read (for thou can'st read) the lay,
  Graved on the stone beneath yon aged thorn.'

(There scattered oft, the earliest of the year,
  By hands unseen, are showers of violets found:
The redbreast loves to bill and warble there,
  And little footsteps lightly print the ground.)

THE EPITAPH

Here rests his head upon the lap of Earth
  A Youth, to Fortune and to Fame unknown.
Fair Science frowned not on his humble birth,
  And Melancholy marked him for her own.

Large was his bounty, and his soul sincere,
  Heaven did a recompense as largely send;
He gave to Misery all he had, a tear,
  He gained from Heaven ('twas all he wished) a friend.

No farther seek his merits to disclose,
  Or draw his frailties from their dread abode,
(There they alike in trembling hope repose,)
  The bosom of his Father and his God.

DYLAN THOMAS 1914–53

FERN HILL

Now as I was young and easy under the apple boughs
About the lilting house and happy as the grass was green,
   The night above the dingle starry,
     Time let me hail and climb
   Golden in the heydays of his eyes,
And honoured among wagons I was prince of the apple towns
And once below a time I lordly had the trees and leaves
     Trail with daisies and barley
   Down the rivers of the windfall light.

And as I was green and carefree, famous among the barns
About the happy yard and singing as the farm was home,
   In the sun that is young once only,
     Time let me play and be
   Golden in the mercy of his means,
And green and golden I was huntsman and herdsman, the calves
Sang to my horn, the foxes on the hills barked clear and cold,
     And the sabbath rang slowly
   In the pebbles of the holy streams.

All the sun long it was running, it was lovely, the hay
Fields high as the house, the tunes from the chimneys, it was air
   And playing, lovely and watery
     And fire green as grass.
   And nightly under the simple stars
As I rode to sleep the owls were bearing the farm away,
All the moon long I heard, blessed among stables, the night-jars
     Flying with the ricks, and the horses
     Flashing into the dark.

And then to awake, and the farm, like a wanderer white
With the dew, come back, the cock on his shoulder: it was all
   Shining, it was Adam and maiden,
     The sky gathered again
   And the sun grew round that very day,
So it must have been after the birth of the simple light

In the first, spinning place, the spellbound horses walking warm
Out of the whinnying green stable
On to the fields of praise.

And honoured among foxes and pheasants by the gay house
Under the new made clouds and happy as the heart was long,
In the sun born over and over,
I ran my heedless ways,
My wishes raced through the house high hay
And nothing I cared, at my sky blue trades, that time allows
In all his tuneful turning so few and such morning songs
Before the children green and golden
Follow him out of grace.

Nothing I cared, in the lamb white days, that time would take me
Up to the swallow thronged loft by the shadow of my hand,
In the moon that is always rising,
Nor that riding to sleep
I should hear him fly with the high fields
And wake to the farm forever fled from the childless land.
Oh as I was young and easy in the mercy of his means,
Time held me green and dying
Though I sang in my chains like the sea.

WILLIAM HENRY DAVIES 1871–1940

LEISURE

What is this life if, full of care,
We have no time to stand and stare.

No time to stand beneath the boughs
And stare as long as sheep or cows.

No time to see, when woods we pass,
Where squirrels hide their nuts in grass.

No time to see, in broad daylight,
Streams full of stars, like skies at night.

No time to turn at Beauty's glance,
And watch her feet, how they can dance.

No time to wait till her mouth can
Enrich that smile her eyes began.

A poor life this if, full of care,
We have no time to stand and stare.

ALFRED NOYES 1880–1959

THE HIGHWAYMAN

The wind was a torrent of darkness among the gusty trees,
The moon was a ghostly galleon tossed upon cloudy seas,
The road was a ribbon of moonlight over the purple moor,
And the highwayman came riding –
        Riding – riding –
The highwayman came riding, up to the old inn-door.

He'd a French cocked-hat on his forehead, a bunch of lace at
    his chin,
A coat of claret velvet, and breeches of brown doe-skin;
They fitted with never a wrinkle: his boots were up to the
    thigh!
And he rode with a jewelled twinkle,
        His pistol butts a-twinkle,
His rapier hilt a-twinkle, under the jewelled sky.

Over the cobbles he clattered and clashed in the dark inn-yard,
And he tapped with his whip on the shutters, but all was
    locked and barred;
He whistled a tune to the window, and who should be waiting
    there
But the landlord's black-eyed daughter,
        Bess, the landlord's daughter,
Plaiting a dark red love-knot into her long black hair.

And dark in the old inn-yard a stable-wicket creaked
Where Tim the ostler listened; his face was white and peaked;
His eyes were hollows of madness, his hair like mouldy hay,
But he loved the landlord's daughter,
        The landlord's red-lipped daughter;
Dumb as a dog he listened, and he heard the robber say –

'One kiss, my bonny sweetheart, I'm after a prize to-night,
But I shall be back with the yellow gold before the morning
    light;
Yet, if they press me sharply, and harry me through the day,
Then look for me by moonlight,

Watch for me by moonlight,
I'll come to thee by moonlight, though hell should bar the way.'

He rose upright in the stirrups; he scarce could reach her hand,
But she loosened her hair i' the casement! His face burnt like a
    brand
As the black cascade of perfume came tumbling over his breast;
And he kissed its waves in the moonlight,
        (Oh, sweet black waves in the moonlight!)
Then he tugged at his rein in the moonlight, and galloped away to
    the west.

II

He did not come in the dawning; he did not come at noon;
And out o' the tawny sunset, before the rise o' the moon,
When the road was a gipsy's ribbon, looping the purple moor,
A red-coat troop came marching –
        Marching – marching –
King George's men came marching, up to the old inn-door.

They said no word to the landlord, they drank his ale instead,
But they gagged his daughter and bound her to the foot of her
    narrow bed;
Two of them knelt at her casement, with muskets at their side!
There was death at every window;
        And hell at one dark window;
For Bess could see, through her casement, the road that *he* would
    ride.
They had tied her up to attention, with many a sniggering jest;
They had bound a musket beside her, with the barrel beneath her
    breast!
'Now keep good watch!' and they kissed her.
        She heard the dead man say –
Look for me by moonlight;
        Watch for me by moonlight;
I'll come to thee by moonlight, though hell should bar the way!

She twisted her hands behind her; but all the knots held good!
She writhed her hands till her fingers were wet with sweat or blood!
They stretched and strained in the darkness, and the hours crawled by
 like years,
Till, now, on the stroke of midnight,
    Cold, on the stroke of midnight,
The tip of one finger touched it! The trigger at least was hers!

The tip of one finger touched it; she strove no more for the rest!
Up, she stood to attention, with the barrel beneath her breast,
She would not risk their hearing; she would not strive again;
For the road lay bare in the moonlight;
    Blank and bare in the moonlight;
And the blood of her veins in the moonlight throbbed to her love's
 refrain.

Tlot-tlot; tloy-tlot! Had they heard it? The horse-hoofs ringing clear;
Tlot-tlot, tlot-tlot, in the distance? Were they deaf that they did not
 hear?
Down the ribbon of moonlight, over the brow of the hill,
The highwayman came riding,
    Riding, riding!
The red-coats looked to their priming! She stood up, straight and still!

Tlot-tlot, in the frosty silence! *tlot-tlot,* in the echoing night!
Nearer he came and nearer! Her face was like a light!
Her eyes grew wide for a moment; she drew one last deep breath,
Then her finger moved in the moonlight,
    Her musket shattered the moonlight,
Shattered her breast in the moonlight and warned him – with her death.

He turned; he spurred to the westward; he did not know who stood
Bowed, with her head o'er the musket, drenched with her own red
 blood!
Not till the dawn he heard it, and slowly blanched to hear
How Bess, the landlord's daughter,
    The landlord's black-eyed daughter,

Had watched for her love in the moonlight, and died in the darkness there.

Back, he spurred like a madman, shrieking a curse to the sky,
With the white road smoking behind him and his rapier brandished high!
Blood-red were his spurs i' the golden noon; wine-red was his velvet coat;
When they shot him down on the highway,
    Down like a dog on the highway,
And he lay in his blood on the highway, with the bunch of lace at his throat.

And still of a winter's night, they say, when the wind is in the trees,
When the moon is a ghostly galleon tossed upon cloudy seas,
When the road is a ribbon of moonlight over the purple moor,
A highwayman comes riding –
    Riding – riding –
A highwayman comes riding, up to the old inn-door.

Over the cobbles he clatters and clangs in the dark inn-yard
And he taps with his whip on the shutters, but all is locked and barred;
He whistles a tune to the window, and who should be waiting there
But the landlord's black-eyed daughter,
    Bess, the landlord's daughter,
Plaiting a dark red love-knot into her long black hair.

16

ANDREW MARVELL 1621-78

TO HIS COY MISTRESS

Had we but world enough, and time,
This coyness, Lady, were no crime
We would sit down and think which way
To walk and pass our long love's day.
Thou by the Indian Ganges' side
Should'st rubies find: I by the tide
Of Humber would complain. I would
Love you ten years before the Flood,
And you should, if you please, refuse
Till the conversion of the Jews.
My vegetable love should grow
Vaster than empires, and more slow.
An hundred years should go to praise
Thine eyes and on thy forehead gaze;
Two hundred to adore each breast,
But thirty thousand to the rest.
An age at least to every part,
And the last age should show your heart.
For, Lady, you deserve this state,
Nor would I love at lower rate.
    But at my back I always hear
Time's wingèd chariot hurrying near;
And yonder all before us lie
Deserts of vast eternity.
Thy beauty shall no more be found,
Nor, in my marble vault, shall sound
My echoing song: then worms shall try
That long preserved virginity,
And your quaint honour turn to dust,
And into ashes all my lust.
The grave's a fine and private place,
But none, I think, do there embrace.
    Now therefore, while the youthful hue
Sits on thy skin like morning dew,
And while thy willing soul transpires

At every pore with instant fires,
Now let us sport us while we may,
And now, like amorous birds of prey,
Rather at once our time devour
Than languish in his slow-chapt power.
Let us roll all our strength and all
Our sweetness up into one ball,
And tear our pleasures with rough strife
Through the iron gates of life:
Thus, though we cannot make our sun
Stand still, yet we will make him run.

MATTHEW ARNOLD 1822–88

DOVER BEACH

The sea is calm to-night.
The tide is full, the moon lies fair
Upon the straits; – on the French coast the light
Gleams and is gone; the cliffs of England stand,
Glimmering and vast, out in the tranquil bay.
Come to the window, sweet is the night-air!
Only, from the long line of spray
Where the sea meets the moon-blanch'd land,
Listen! you hear the grating roar
Of pebbles which the waves draw back, and fling,
At their return, up the high strand,
Begin, and cease, and then again begin,
With tremulous cadence slow, and bring
The eternal note of sadness in.

Sophocles long ago
Heard it on the Aegean, and it brought
Into his mind the turbid ebb and flow
Of human misery; we
Find also in the sound a thought,
Hearing it by this distant northern sea.

The Sea of Faith
Was once, too, at the full, and round earth's shore
Lay like the folds of a bright girdle furl'd.
But now I only hear
Its melancholy, long, withdrawing roar,
Retreating, to the breath
Of the night-wind, down the vast edges drear
And naked shingles of the world.

Ah, love, let us be true
To one another! for the world, which seems
To lie before us like a land of dreams,
So various, so beautiful, so new,
Hath really neither joy, nor love, nor light,

Nor certitude, nor peace, nor help for pain;
And we are here as on a darkling plain
Swept with confused alarms of struggle and flight.
Where ignorant armies clash by night.

WILLIAM BLAKE 1757–1827

THE TYGER

Tyger! Tyger! burning bright
In the forests of the night,
What immortal hand or eye
Could frame thy fearful symmetry?

In what distant deeps or skies
Burnt the fire of thine eyes?
On what wings dare he aspire?
What the hand dare seize the fire?

And what shoulder, & what art,
Could twist the sinews of thy heart?
And when thy heart began to beat,
What dread hand? & what dread feet?

What the hammer? what the chain?
In what furnace was thy brain?
What the anvil? what dread grasp
Dare its deadly terrors clasp?

When the stars threw down their spears,
And water'd heaven with their tears,
Did he smile his work to see?
Did he who made the Lamb make thee?

Tyger! Tyger! burning bright
In the forest of the night,
What immortal hand or eye,
Dare frame thy fearful symmetry?

W.H. AUDEN 1907–73

TWELVE SONGS

IX

Stop all the clocks, cut off the telephone,
Prevent the dog from barking with a juicy bone,
Silence the pianos and with muffled drum
Bring out the coffin, let the mourners come.

Let aeroplanes circle moaning overhead
Scribbling on the sky the message He Is Dead,
Put crêpe bows round the white necks of the
        public doves,
Let the traffic policemen wear black cotton gloves.

He was my North, my South, my East and West,
My working week and my Sunday rest,
My noon, my midnight, my talk, my song;
I thought that love would last for ever: I was wrong.

The stars are not wanted now: put out every one;
Pack up the moon and dismantle the sun;
Pour away the ocean and sweep up the wood.
For nothing now can ever come to any good.

20

EDWARD THOMAS 1878–1917

ADLESTROP

Yes. I remember Adlestrop –
The name, because one afternoon
Of heat the express-train drew up there
Unwontedly. It was late June.

The steam hissed. Some one cleared his throat.
No one left and no one came
On the bare platform. What I saw
Was Adlestrop – only the name

And willows, willow-herb, and grass,
And meadowsweet, and haycocks dry,
No whit less still and lonely fair
Than the high cloudlets in the sky.

And for that minute a blackbird sang
Close by, and around him, mistier,
Farther and farther, all the birds
Of Oxfordshire and Gloucestershire.

RUPERT BROOKE 1887–1915

THE SOLDIER

If I should die, think only this of me:
  That there's some corner of a foreign field
That is for ever England. There shall be
  In that rich earth a richer dust concealed;
A dust whom England bore, shaped, made aware,
  Gave, once her flowers to love, her ways to roam,
A body of England's, breathing English air,
  Washed by the rivers, blessed by the suns of home.

And think, this heart, all evil shed away,
  A pulse in the eternal mind, no less
    Gives somewhere back the thoughts by England given;
Her sights and sounds; dreams happy as her day;
  And laughter, learnt of friends; and gentleness,
    In hearts a peace, under an English heaven.

JENNY JOSEPH 1932–

WARNING

When I am an old woman I shall wear purple
With a red hat which doesn't go, and doesn't suit me,
And I shall spend my pension on brandy and summer gloves
And satin sandals, and say we've no money for butter.
I shall sit down on the pavement when I'm tired
And gobble up samples in shops and press alarm bells
And run my stick along the public railings
And make up for the sobriety of my youth.
I shall go out in my slippers in the rain
And pick the flowers in other people's gardens
And learn to spit.

You can wear terrible shirts and grow more fat
And eat three pounds of sausages at a go
Or only bread and pickle for a week
And hoard pens and pencils and beermats and things in boxes.

But now we must have clothes that keep us dry
And pay our rent and not swear in the street
And set a good example for the children.
We must have friends to dinner and read the papers.

But maybe I ought to practise a little now?
So people who know me are not too shocked and surprised
When suddenly I am old, and start to wear purple.

23

JOHN MASEFIELD 1878–1967

SEA-FEVER

I must go down to the seas again, to the lonely sea and the sky,
And all I ask is a tall ship and a star to steer her by,
And the wheel's kick and the wind's song and the white sail's
    shaking,
And a grey mist on the sea's face and a grey dawn breaking.

I must go down to the seas again, for the call of the running tide
Is a wild call and a clear call that may not be denied;
And all I ask is a windy day with the white clouds flying,
And the flung spray and the blown spume, and the sea-gulls
    crying.

I must go down to the seas again, to the vagrant gypsy life,
To the gull's way and the whale's way where the wind's like a
    whetted knife;
And all I ask is a merry yarn from a laughing fellow-rover,
And quiet sleep and a sweet dream when the long trick's over.

24

WILLIAM WORDSWORTH 1770–1850

UPON WESTMINSTER BRIDGE

Sept. 3, 1802

Earth has not anything to show more fair:
Dull would he be of soul who could pass by
A sight so touching in its majesty:
This City now doth like a garment wear

The beauty of the morning: silent, bare,
Ships, towers, domes, theatres, and temples lie
Open unto the fields, and to the sky,
All bright and glittering in the smokeless air.

Never did sun more beautifully steep
In his first splendour valley, rock, or hill;
Ne'er saw I, never felt, a calm so deep!

The river glideth at his own sweet will:
Dear God! the very houses seem asleep;
And all that mighty heart is lying still!

ELIZABETH BARRETT BROWNING 1806–61

SONNETS FROM THE PORTUGUESE

XLIII

How do I love thee? Let me count the ways.
I love thee to the depth and breadth and height
My soul can reach, when feeling out of sight
For the ends of Being and ideal Grace.
I love thee to the level of everyday's
Most quiet need, by sun and candlelight.
I love thee freely, as men strive for Right;
I love thee purely, as they turn from Praise.
I love thee with the passion put to use
In my old griefs, and with my childhood's faith.
I love thee with a love I seemed to lose
With my lost saints, – I love thee with the breath,
Smiles, tears, of all my life! – and, if God choose,
I shall but love thee better after death.

T.S. ELIOT 1885–1965

THE LOVE SONG OF J. ALFRED PRUFROCK

S'io credessi che mia risposta fosse
a persona che mai tornasse al mondo,
questa fiamma staria senza più scosse.
Ma per ciò che giammai di questo fondo
non tornò vivo alcun, s'i'odo il vero,
senza tema d'infamia ti rispondo.

Let us go then, you and I,
When the evening is spread out against the sky
Like a patient etherised upon a table;
Let us go, through certain half-deserted streets,
The muttering retreats
Of restless nights in one-night cheap hotels
And sawdust restaurants with oyster-shells:
Streets that follow like a tedious argument
Of insidious intent
To lead you to an overwhelming question ...
Oh, do not ask, 'What is it?'
Let us go and make our visit.

In the room the women come and go
Talking of Michelangelo.

The yellow fog that rubs its back upon the window-panes,
The yellow smoke that rubs its muzzle on the window-panes,
Licked its tongue into the corners of the evening,
Lingered upon the pools that stand in drains,
Let fall upon its back the soot that falls from chimneys,
Slipped by the terrace, made a sudden leap,
And seeing that it was a soft October night,
Curled once about the house, and fell asleep.

And indeed there will be time
For the yellow smoke that slides along the street
Rubbing its back upon the window-panes;
There will be time, there will be time
To prepare a face to meet the faces that you meet;

There will be time to murder and create,
And time for all the works and days of hands
That lift and drop a question on your plate;
Time for you and time for me,
And time yet for a hundred indecisions,
And for a hundred visions and revisions,
Before the taking of a toast and tea.

In the room the women come and go
Talking of Michelangelo.

And indeed there will be time
To wonder, 'Do I dare?' and, 'Do I dare?'
Time to turn back and descend the stair,
With a bald spot in the middle of my hair –
(They will say: 'How his hair is growing thin!')
My morning coat, my collar mounting firmly to the chin,
My necktie rich and modest, but asserted by a simple pin –
(They will say: 'But how his arms and legs are thin!')
Do I dare
Disturb the universe?
In a minute there is time
For decisions and revisions which a minute will reverse.

For I have known them all already, known them all –
Have known the evenings, mornings, afternoons,
I have measured out my life with coffee spoons;
I know the voices dying with a dying fall
Beneath the music from a farther room.
So how should I presume?

And I have known the eyes already, known them all –
The eyes that fix you in a formulated phrase,
And when I am formulated, sprawling on a pin,
When I am pinned and wriggling on the wall,
Then how should I begin
To spit out all the butt-ends of my days and ways?
And how should I presume?

And I have known the arms already, known them all –
Arms that are braceleted and white and bare
(But in the lamplight, downed with light brown hair!)
Is it perfume from a dress

That makes me so digress?
Arms that lie along a table, or wrap about a shawl.
　And should I then presume?
　And how should I begin?

　　　.　　.　　.　　.　　.

　Shall I say, I have gone at dusk through narrow streets
And watched the smoke that rises from the pipes
Of lonely men in shirt-sleeves, leaning out of windows? ...

　I should have been a pair of ragged claws
Scuttling across the floors of silent seas.

　　　.　　.　　.　　.　　.

　And the afternoons, the evening, sleeps so peacefully!
Smoothed by long fingers,
Asleep ... tired ... or it malingers,
Stretched on the floor, here beside you and me.
Should I, after tea and cakes and ices,
Have the strength to force the moment to its crisis?
But though I have wept and fasted, wept and prayed,
Though I have seen my head (grown slightly bald)
　　brought in upon a platter,
I am no prophet – and here's no great matter;
I have seen the moment of my greatness flicker,
and I have seen the eternal Footman hold my coat, and
　　snicker,
And in short, I was afraid.

　And would it have been worth it, after all,
After the cups, the marmalade, the tea,
Among the porcelain, among some talk of you and me,
Would it have been worth while,
To have bitten off the matter with a smile,
To have squeezed the universe into a ball
To roll it towards some overwhelming question,
To say: 'I am Lazarus, come from the dead,
Come back to tell you all, I shall tell you all' –
If one, settling a pillow by her head,
　　Should say: 'That is not what I meant at all.
　　That is not it, at all.'

And would it have been worth it, after all,
Would it have been worth while,
After the sunsets and the dooryards and the sprinkled
    streets,
After the novels, after the teacups, after the skirts that
    trail along the floor –
And this, and so much more? –
It is impossible to say just what I mean!
But as if a magic lantern threw the nerves in patterns on a
    screen:
Would it have been worth while
If one, settling a pillow or throwing off a shawl,
And turning toward the window, should say:
    'That is not it at all,
    That is not what I meant at all.'

     .   .   .   .   .

No! I am not Prince Hamlet, nor was meant to be;
Am an attendant lord, one that will do
To swell a progress, start a scene or two,
Advise the prince; no doubt, an easy tool,
Deferential, glad to be of use,
Politic, cautious, and meticulous;
Full of high sentence, but a bit obtuse;
At times, indeed, almost ridiculous –
Almost, at times, the Fool.

I grow old … I grow old …
I shall wear the bottoms of my trousers rolled.

Shall I part my hair behind? Do I dare eat a peach?
I shall wear white flannel trousers, and walk upon the beach.
I have heard the mermaids singing, each to each.

I do not think that they will sing to me.

I have seen them riding seaward on the waves
Combing the white hair of the waves blown back
When the wind blows the water white and black.

We have lingered in the chambers of the sea
By sea-girls wreathed with seaweed red and brown
Till human voices wake us, and we drown.

JOHN MASEFIELD 1878-1967

CARGOES

Quinquireme of Nineveh from distant Ophir
Rowing home to haven in sunny Palestine,
With a cargo of ivory,
And apes and peacocks,
Sandalwood, cedarwood, and sweet white wine.

Stately Spanish galleon coming from the Isthmus,
Dipping through the Tropics by the palm-green shores,
With a cargo of diamonds,
Emeralds, amethysts,
Topazes, and cinnamon and gold moidores.

Dirty British coaster with a salt-caked smoke stack
Butting through the Channel in the mad March days,
With a cargo of Tyne coal,
Road-rail, pig-lead,
Firewood, iron-ware, and cheap tin trays.

LEWIS CARROLL 1832–98

JABBERWOCKY

'Twas brillig, and the slithy toves
  Did gyre and gimble in the wabe;
All mimsy were the borogoves,
  And the mome raths outgrabe.

'Beware the Jabberwock, my son!
  The jaws that bite, the claws that catch!
Beware the Jubjub bird, and shun
  The frumious Bandersnatch!'

He took his vorpal sword in hand:
  Long time the manxome foe he sought –
So rested he by the Tumtum tree,
  And stood awhile in thought.

And as in uffish thought he stood,
  The Jabberwock, with eyes of flame,
Came whiffling through the tulgey wood,
  And burbled as it came!

One, two! One, two! And through and through
  The vorpal blade went snicker-snack!
He left it dead, and with its head
  He went galumphing back.

'And thou hast slain the Jabberwock?
  Come to my arms, my beamish boy!
O frabjous day! Callooh! Callay!'
  He chortled in his joy.

'Twas brillig, and the slithy toves
  Did gyre and gimble in the wabe;
All mimsy were the borogoves,
  And the mome raths outgrabe.

SAMUEL TAYLOR COLERIDGE 1772–1834

from THE RIME OF THE ANCIENT MARINER

PART 1

It is an ancient Mariner,
And he stoppeth one of three.
'By thy long grey beard and glittering eye,
Now wherefore stopp'st thou me?

The Bridegroom's doors are opened wide.
And I am next of kin;
The guests are met, the feast is set:
May'st hear the merry din.'

He holds him with his skinny hand.
'There was a ship,' quoth he.
'Hold off! unhand me, grey-beard loon!'
Eftsoons his hand dropt he.

He holds him with his glittering eye –
The Wedding-Guest stood still.
And listens like a three years' child:
The Mariner hath his will.

The Wedding-Guest sat on a stone:
He cannot choose but hear:
And thus spake on that ancient man.
The bright-eyed Mariner.

'The ship was cheered, the harbour cleared,
Merrily did we drop
Below the kirk, below the hill,
Below the lighthouse top.

The Sun came up upon the left,
Out of the sea came he!
And he shone bright, and on the right
Went down into the sea.

Higher and higher every day,
Till over the mast at noon –'

The Wedding-Guest here beat his breast,
For he heard the loud bassoon.

The bride hath paced into the hall,
Red as a rose is she;
Nodding their heads before her goes
The merry minstrelsy.

The Wedding-Guest he beat his breast,
Yet he cannot choose but hear;
And thus spake on that ancient man,
The bright-eyed Mariner.
'And now STORM-BLAST came, and he
Was tyrannous and strong:
He struck with his o'ertaking wings,
And chased us south along.

With sloping masts and dipping prow,
As who pursued with yell and blow
Still treads the shadow of his foe,
And forward bends his head,
The ship drove fast, loud roared the blast,
And southward aye we fled.

And now there came both mist and snow,
And it grew wondrous cold:
And ice, mast-high, came floating by,
As green as emerald.

And through the drifts the snowy clifts
Did send a dismal sheen:
Nor shapes of men nor beasts we ken –
The ice was all between.

The ice was here, the ice was there,
The ice was all around:
It cracked and growled, and roared and howled,
Like noises in a swound!

At length did cross an Albatross,
Thorough the fog it came;
As if it had been a Christian soul,
We hailed it in God's name.

It ate the food it ne'er had eat,
And round and round it flew.
The ice did split with a thunder-fit;
The helmsman steered us through!

And a good south wind sprung up behind;
The Albatross did follow,
And every day, for food or play,
Came to the mariner's hollo!

In mist or cloud, on mast or shroud,
It perched for vespers nine;
Whiles all the night, through fog-smoke white,
Glimmered the white Moon-shine.'

'God save thee, ancient Mariner!
From the fiends, that plague thee thus! –
Why look'st thou so?' – 'With my cross-bow
I shot the Albatross.'

PERCY BYSSHE SHELLEY 1792–1822

OZYMANDIAS OF EGYPT

I met a traveller from an antique land
Who said: Two vast and trunkless legs of stone
Stand in the desert. Near them on the sand,
Half sunk, a shatter'd visage lies, whose frown
And wrinkled lip and sneer of cold command
Tell that its sculptor well those passions read
Which yet survive, stamp'd on these lifeless things,
The hand that mock'd them and the heart that fed;
And on the pedestal these words appear:
'My name is Ozymandias, king of kings:
Look on my works, ye Mighty, and despair!'
Nothing beside remains. Round the decay
Of that colossal wreck, boundless and bare,
The lone and level sands stretch far away.

ROBERT FROST 1874–1963

STOPPING BY WOODS ON A SNOWY EVENING

Whose woods these are I think I know.
His house is in the village though;
He will not see me stopping here
To watch his woods fill up with snow.

My little horse must think it queer
To stop without a farmhouse near
Between the woods and frozen lake
The darkest evening of the year.

He gives his harness bells a shake
To ask if there is some mistake.
The only other sound's the sweep
Of easy wind and downy flake.

The woods are lovely, dark and deep.
But I have promises to keep,
And miles to go before I sleep,
And miles to go before I sleep.

LEIGH HUNT 1784–1859

ABOU BEN ADHEM

Abou Ben Adhem (may his tribe increase!)
Awoke one night from a deep dream of peace,
And saw, within the moonlight in his room,
Making it rich, and like a lily bloom,
An angel writing in a book of gold:
Exceeding peace had made Ben Adhem bold,
And to the presence in the room he said,
'What writest thou?' The vision raised its head,
And with a look made of all sweet accord,
Answered, 'The names of those who love the Lord.'
'And is mine one?' said Abou. 'Nay, not so,'
Replied the angel. Abou spoke more low,
But cheerly still; and said, 'I pray thee, then,
Write me as one that loves his fellow men.'
The angel wrote, and vanished. The next night
It came again with a great wakening light,
And showed the names who love of God had blest,
And lo! Ben Adhem's name led all the rest.

33

SIEGFRIED SASSOON 1886–1967

EVERYONE SANG

Everyone suddenly burst out singing;
And I was filled with such delight
As prisoned birds must find in freedom
Winging wildly across the white
Orchards and dark-green fields; on; on; and out of sight.

Everyone's voice was suddenly lifted,
And beauty came like the setting sun.
My heart was shaken with tears; and horror
Drifted away ... O but every one
Was a bird; and the song was wordless; the singing
    will never be done.

GERARD MANLEY HOPKINS 1844-89

THE WINDHOVER

To Christ our Lord

I caught this morning morning's minion kingdom
   of daylight's dauphin, dapple-dawn-drawn Falcon, in
      his riding
   Of the rolling level underneath him steady air, and striding
High there, how he rung upon the rein of a wimpling wing
In his ecstasy! then off, off forth on swing,
   As a skate's heel sweeps smooth on a bow-bend: the hurl
      and gliding
   Rebuffed the big wind. My heart in hiding
Stirred for a bird, – the achieve of, the mastery of the thing!

Brute beauty and valour and act, oh, air, pride, plume, here
   Buckle! AND the fire that breaks from thee then, a billion
Times told lovelier, more dangerous, O my chevalier!

   No wonder of it: shèer plòd makes plough down sillion
Shine, and blue-bleak embers, ah my dear,
   Fall, gall themselves, and gash gold vermilion.

DYLAN THOMAS 1914–53

DO NOT GO GENTLE INTO THAT GOOD NIGHT

Do not go gentle into that good night,
Old age should burn and rave at close of day;
Rage, rage against the dying of the light.

Though wise men at their end know dark is right,
Because their words had forked no lightning they
Do not go gentle into that good night.

Good men, the last wave by, crying how bright
Their frail deeds might have danced in a green bay,
Rage, rage against the dying of the light.

Wild men who caught and sang the sun in flight,
And learn, too late, they grieved it on its way,
Do not go gentle into that good night.

Grave men, near death, who see with blinding sight
Blind eyes could blaze like meteors and be gay,
Rage, rage against the dying of the light.

And you, my father, there on the sad height,
Curse, bless, me now with your fierce tears, I pray.
Do not go gentle into that good night.
Rage, rage against the dying of the light.

WILLIAM SHAKESPEARE 1564–1616

SONNET 18

Shall I compare thee to a summer's day?
Thou art more lovely and more temperate:
Rough winds do shake the darling buds of May,
And summer's lease hath all too short a date:
Sometime too hot the eye of heaven shines,
And often is his gold complexion dimm'd,
And every fair from fair sometime declines,
By chance or natures changing course untrimm'd:
But thy eternal summer shall not fade,
Nor lose possession of that fair thou owest,
Nor shall death brag thou wandrest in his shade,
When in eternal lines to time thou growest,
   So long as men can breathe or eyes can see
   So long lives this, and this gives life to thee.

37

W.B. YEATS 1865–1939

WHEN YOU ARE OLD

When you are old and grey and full of sleep,
And nodding by the fire, take down this book,
And slowly read, and dream of the soft look
Your eyes had once, and of their shadows deep;

How many loved your moments of glad grace,
And loved your beauty with love false or true,
But one man loved the pilgrim soul in you,
And loved the sorrows of your changing face;

And bending down beside the glowing bars,
Murmur, a little sadly, how Love fled
And paced upon the mountains overhead
And hid his face amid a crowd of stars.

HENRY REED 1914–86

LESSONS OF THE WAR (TO ALAN MICHELL)

Vixi duellis nuper idoneus
Et militavi non sine gloria

1. NAMING OF PARTS.

To-day we have naming of parts. Yesterday,
We had daily cleaning. And to-morrow morning,
We shall have what to do after firing. But to-day,
To-day we have naming of parts. Japonica
Glistens like coral in all of the neighbouring gardens,
    And to-day we have naming of parts.

This is the lower sling swivel. And this
Is the upper sling swivel, whose use you will see,
When you are given your slings. And this is the piling swivel,
Which in your case you have not got. The branches
Hold in the gardens their silent, eloquent gestures,
    Which in our case we have not got.

This is the safety-catch, which is always released
With an easy flick of the thumb. And please do not let me
See anyone using his finger. You can do it quite easy
If you have any strength in your thumb. The blossoms
Are fragile and motionless, never letting anyone see
    Any of them using their finger.

And this you can see is the bolt. The purpose of this
Is to open the breech, as you see. We can slide it
Rapidly backwards and forwards: we call this
Easing the spring. And rapidly backwards and forwards
The early bees are assaulting and fumbling the flowers:
    They call it easing the Spring.

They call it easing the Spring; it is perfectly easy
If you have any strength in your thumb; like the bolt,
And the breech, and the cocking-piece, and the point of balance,
Which in our case we have not got; and the almond blossom
Silent in all of the gardens and the bees going backwards and forwards,
    For to-day we have naming of parts.

THOMAS HARDY 1840–1928

THE DARKLING THRUSH

I leant upon a coppice gate
    When Frost was spectre-gray,
And Winter's dregs made desolate
    The weakening eye of day.
The tangled bine-stems scored the sky
    Like strings of broken lyres,
And all mankind that haunted nigh
    Had sought their household fires.

The land's sharp features seemed to be
    The Century's corpse outleant,
His crypt the cloudy canopy,
    The wind his death-lament.
The ancient pulse of germ and birth
    Was shrunken hard and dry,
And every spirit upon earth
    Seemed fervourless as I.

At once a voice arose among
    The bleak twigs overhead
In a full-hearted evensong
    Of joy illimited;
An aged thrush, frail, gaunt, and small,
    In blast-beruffled plume,
Had chosen thus to fling his soul
    Upon the growing gloom.

So little cause for carolings
    Of such ecstatic sound
Was written on terrestrial things
    Afar or nigh around,
That I could think there trembled through
    His happy good-night air
Some blessed Hope, whereof he knew
    And I was unaware.

ALLAN AHLBERG 1938–

PLEASE MRS BUTLER

Please Mrs Butler
This boy Derek Drew
Keeps copying my work, Miss.
What shall I do?

Go and sit in the hall, dear.
Go and sit in the sink.
Take your books on the roof, my lamb.
Do whatever you think.

Please Mrs Butler
This boy Derek Drew
Keeps taking my rubber, Miss.
What shall I do?

Keep it in your hand, dear.
Hide it up your vest.
Swallow it if you like, my love.
Do what you think best.

Please Mrs Butler
This boy Derek Drew
Keeps calling me rude names, Miss.
What shall I do?

Lock yourself in the cupboard, dear.
Run away to sea.
Do whatever you can, my flower.
But *don't ask me*!

SAMUEL TAYLOR COLERIDGE 1772–1834

KUBLA KHAN

In Xanadu did Kubla Khan
A stately pleasure-dome decree:
Where Alph, the sacred river, ran
Through caverns measureless to man
   Down to a sunless sea.
So twice five miles of fertile ground
With walls and towers girdled round:
And here were gardens bright with sinuous rills,
Where blossomed many an incense-bearing tree;
And here were forests ancient as the hills
Enfolding sunny spots of greenery.

But oh! that deep romantic chasm which slanted
Down the green hill athwart a cedarn cover!
A savage place! as holy and enchanted
As e'er beneath a waning moon was haunted
By woman wailing for her demon-lover!
And from this chasm, with ceaseless turmoil seething,
As if this earth in fast thick pants were breathing,
A mighty fountain momently was forced:
Amid whose swift half-intermitted burst
Huge fragments vaulted like rebounding hail,
Or chaffy grain beneath the thresher's flail;
And 'mid these dancing rocks at once and ever
It flung up momently the sacred river.
Five miles meandering with a mazy motion
Through wood and dale the sacred river ran,
Then reached the caverns measureless to man,
And sank in tumult to a lifeless ocean:
And 'mid this tumult Kubla heard from afar
Ancestral voices prophesying war!

   The shadow of the dome of pleasure
   Floated midway on the waves;
   Where was heard the mingled measure
   From the fountain and the caves.

It was a miracle of rare device,
A sunny pleasure-dome with caves of ice!

    A damsel with a dulcimer
    In a vision once I saw:
    It was an Abyssinian maid,
    And on her dulcimer she played,
    Singing of Mount Abora.
    Could I revive within me
    Her symphony and song,
    To such a deep delight 'twould win me,
That with music loud and long,
I would build that dome in air,
That sunny dome! those caves of ice!
And all who heard should see them there,
And all should cry, Beware! Beware!
His flashing eyes, his floating hair!
Weave a circle round him thrice,
And close your eyes with holy dread,
For he on honey-dew hath fed,
And drunk the milk of Paradise.

42

ROBERT BROWNING 1812-89

HOME-THOUGHTS, FROM ABROAD

Oh, to be in England
Now that April's there,
And whoever wakes in England
Sees, some morning, unaware,
That the lowest boughs and the brushwood sheaf
Round the elm-tree bole are in tiny leaf,
While the chaffinch sings on the orchard bough
In England – now!

And after April, when May follows,
And the whitethroat builds, and all the swallows –
Hark! where my blossomed pear-tree in the hedge
Leans to the field and scatters on the clover
Blossoms and dewdrops – at the bent spray's edge –
That's the wise thrush; he sings each song twice over,
Lest you should think he never could recapture
The first fine careless rapture!
And though the fields look rough with hoary dew,
All will be gay when noontide wakes anew
The buttercups, the little children's dower,
– Far brighter than this gaudy melon-flower!

JOHN GILLESPIE MAGEE 1922–41

HIGH FLIGHT (AN AIRMAN'S ECSTASY)

Oh, I have slipped the surly bonds of earth
And danced the skies on laughter-silvered wings;
Sunward I've climbed and joined the tumbling mirth
Of sun-split clouds – and done a hundred things
You have not dreamed of; wheeled and soared and swung
High in the sun-lit silence. Hovering there
I've chased the shouting wind along, and flung
My eager craft through footless halls of air;
Up, up the long, delirious, burning blue
I've topped the wind-swept heights with easy grace,
Where never lark nor even eagle flew;
And while, with silent lifting mind I've trod
The high untrespassed sanctity of space,
Put out my hand, and touched the face of God.

T.S. ELIOT 1885–1965

JOURNEY OF THE MAGI

'A cold coming we had of it,
Just the worst time of the year
For a journey, and such a long journey:
The ways deep and the weather sharp,
The very dead of winter.'
And the camels galled, sore-footed, refractory,
Lying down in the melting snow.
There were times we regretted
The summer palaces on slopes, the terraces,
And the silken girls bringing sherbet.

Then the camel men cursing and grumbling
And running away, and wanting their liquor and women,
And the night-fires going out, and the lack of shelters,
And the cities hostile and the towns unfriendly
And the villages dirty and charging high prices:
A hard time we had of it.
At the end we preferred to travel all night,
Sleeping in snatches,
With the voices singing in our ears, saying
That this was all folly.

Then at dawn we came down to a temperate valley,
Wet, below the snow line, smelling of vegetation,
With a running stream and a water-mill beating the darkness,
And three trees on the low sky.
And an old white horse galloped away in the meadow.
Then we came to a tavern with vine-leaves over the lintel,
Six hands at an open door dicing for pieces of silver,
And feet kicking the empty wine-skins.
But there was no information, and so we continued
And arrived at evening, not a moment too soon
Finding the place; it was (you may say) satisfactory.

All this was a long time ago, I remember,
And I would do it again, but set down

This set down
This: were we led all that way for
Birth or Death? There was a Birth, certainly,
We had evidence and no doubt. I had seen birth and death,
But had thought they were different; this Birth was
Hard and bitter agony for us, like Death, our death.
We returned to our places, these Kingdoms,
But no longer at ease here, in the old dispensation,
With an alien people clutching their gods.
I should be glad of another death.

EDWARD LEAR 1812–88

THE OWL AND THE PUSSY-CAT

The Owl and the Pussy-Cat went to sea
    In a beautiful pea-green boat.
They took some honey, and plenty of money
    Wrapped up in a five-pound note.
The Owl looked up to the stars above,
    And sang to a small guitar,
'O lovely Pussy! O Pussy, my love,
What a beautiful Pussy you are,
        You are,
        You are!
What a beautiful Pussy you are!'

Pussy said to Owl, 'You elegant fowl!
    How charmingly sweet you sing!
O let us be married! too long we have tarried:
    But what shall we do for a ring?'
They sailed away, for a year and a day,
    To the land where the Bong-Tree grows,
And there in a wood a Piggy-wig stood,
With a ring at the end of his nose,
        His nose,
        His nose!
With a ring at the end of his nose.

'Dear Pig, are you willing to sell for one shilling
    Your ring?' Said the Piggy, 'I will.'
So they took it away, and were married next day
    By the Turkey who lives on the hill.
They dinèd on mince, and slices of quince,
    Which they ate with a runcible spoon;
And hand in hand, on the edge of the sand
    They danced by the light of the moon,
        The moon,
        The moon,
They danced by the light of the moon.

RUDYARD KIPLING 1865–1936

THE GLORY OF THE GARDEN

Our England is a garden that is full of stately views,
Of borders, beds and shrubberies and lawns and avenues,
With statues on the terraces and peacocks strutting by;
But the Glory of the Garden lies in more than meets the eye.

For where the old thick laurels grow, along the thin red wall,
You find the tool- and potting-sheds which are the heart of all;
The cold-frames and the hot-houses, the dungpits and the tanks,
The rollers, carts and drain-pipes, with the barrows and the planks.

And there you'll see the gardeners, the man and 'prentice boys
Told off to do as they are bid and do it without noise;
For, except when seeds are planted and we shout to scare the birds,
The Glory of the Garden it abideth not in words.

And some can pot begonias and some can bud a rose,
And some are hardly fit to trust with anything that grows;
But they can roll and trim the lawns and sift the sand and loam,
For the Glory of the Garden occupieth all who come.

Our England is a garden, and such gardens are not made
By singing: – 'Oh, how beautiful!' and sitting in the shade,
While better men than we go out and start their working lives
At grubbing weeds from gravel-paths with broken dinner-knives.

There's not a pair of legs so thin, there's not a head so thick,
There's not a hand so weak and white, nor yet a heart so sick,
But it can find some needful job that's crying to be done,
For the Glory of the Garden glorifieth every one.

Then seek your job with thankfulness and work till further orders,
If it's only netting strawberries or killing slugs on borders;
And when your back stops aching and your hands begin to harden,
You will find yourself a partner in the Glory of the Garden.

Oh, Adam was a gardener, and God who made him sees
That half a proper gardener's work is done upon his knees,
So when your work is finished, you can wash your hands and pray
For the Glory of the Garden, that it may not pass away!
And the Glory of the Garden it shall never pass away!

ROBERT FROST 1874–1963

THE ROAD NOT TAKEN

Two roads diverged in a yellow wood,
And sorry I could not travel both
And be one traveller, long I stood
And looked down one as far as I could
To where it bent in the undergrowth;

Then took the other, as just as fair,
And having perhaps the better claim,
Because it was grassy and wanted wear;
Though as for that the passing there
Had worn them really about the same,

And both that morning equally lay
In leaves no step had trodden black.
Oh, I kept the first for another day!
Yet knowing how way leads on to way,
I doubted if I should ever come back.

I shall be telling this with a sigh
Somewhere ages and ages hence:
Two roads diverged in a wood, and I –
I took the one less travelled by,
And that has made all the difference.

RUDYARD KIPLING 1865–1936

THE WAY THROUGH THE WOODS

'Marklake Witches' – *Rewards and Fairies*

They shut the road through the woods
Seventy years ago.
Weather and rain have undone it again,
And now you would never know
There was once a road through the woods
Before they planted the trees.
It is underneath the coppice and heath
And the thin anemones.
Only the keeper sees
That, where the ring-dove broods,
And the badgers roll at ease,
There was once a road through the woods.

Yet, if you enter the woods
Of a summer evening late,
When the night-air cools on the trout-ringed pools
Where the otter whistles his mate,
(They fear not men in the woods,
Because they see so few.)
You will hear the beat of a horse's feet,
And the swish of a skirt in the dew,
Steadily cantering through
The misty solitudes,
As though they perfectly knew
The old lost road through the woods ...
But there is no road through the woods.

WILFRED OWEN 1893–1918

ANTHEM FOR DOOMED YOUTH

What passing-bells for these who die as cattle?
    Only the monstrous anger of the guns.
    Only the stuttering rifles' rapid rattle
Can patter out their hasty orisons.
No mockeries now for them; no prayers nor bells,
    Nor any voice of mourning save the choirs, –
The shrill, demented choirs of wailing shells;
    And bugles calling for them from sad shires.

What candles may be held to speed them all?
    Not in the hands of boys, but in their eyes
Shall shine the holy glimmers of good-byes.
    The pallor of girls' brows shall be their pall;
Their flowers the tenderness of patient minds,
And each slow dusk a drawing down of blinds.

WENDY COPE 1945–

BLOODY MEN

Bloody men are like bloody buses –
You wait for about a year
And as soon as one approaches your stop
Two or three others appear.

You look at them flashing their indicators,
Offering you a ride.
You're trying to read the destinations,
You haven't much time to decide.

If you make a mistake, there is no turning back.
Jump off, and you'll stand there and gaze
While the cars and the taxis and lorries go by
And the minutes, the hours, the days.

51

JOHN CLARE 1793-1864

EMMONSAIL'S HEATH IN WINTER

I love to see the old heath's withered brake
Mingle its crimpled leaves with furze and ling,
While the old heron from the lonely lake
Starts slow and flaps its melancholy wing,
An oddling crow in idle motion swing
On the half-rotten ash-tree's topmost twig,
Beside whose trunk the gypsy makes his bed.
Up flies the bouncing woodcock from the brig
Where a black quagmire quakes beneath the tread;
The fieldfares chatter in the whistling thorn
And for the haw round fields and closen rove,
And coy bumbarrels, twenty in a drove,
Flit down the hedgerows in the frozen plain
And hang on little twigs and start again.

T.S. ELIOT 1885–1965

LA FIGLIA CHE PIANGE

O quam te memorem virgo –

Stand on the highest pavement of the stair –
Lean on a garden urn –
Weave, weave the sunlight in your hair –
Clasp your flowers to you with a pained surprise –
Fling them to the ground and turn
With a fugitive resentment in your eyes:
But weave, weave the sunlight in your hair.

So I would have had him leave,
So I would have had her stand and grieve,
So he would have left
As the soul leaves the body torn and bruised,
As the mind deserts the body it has used.
I should find
Some way incomparably light and deft,
Some way we both should understand,
Simple and faithless as a smile and shake of the hand.

She turned away, but with the autumn weather
Compelled my imagination many days,
Many days and many hours:
Her hair over her arms and her arms full of flowers.
And I wonder how they should have been together!
I should have lost a gesture and a pose.
Sometimes these cogitations still amaze
The troubled midnight and the noon's repose.

PHILIP LARKIN 1922–80

THE WHITSUN WEDDINGS

That Whitsun, I was late getting away:
  Not till about
One-twenty on the sunlit Saturday
Did my three-quarters-empty train pull out,
All windows down, all cushions hot, all sense
Of being in a hurry gone. We ran
Behind the backs of houses, crossed a street
Of blinding windscreens, smelt the fish-dock thence
The river's level drifting breadth began,
Where sky and Lincolnshire and water meet.

All afternoon, through the tall heat that slept
  For miles inland,
A slow and stopping curve southwards we kept.
Wide farms went by, short-shadowed cattle, and
Canals with floatings of industrial froth;
A hothouse flashed uniquely: hedges dipped
And rose: and now and then a smell of grass
Displaced the reek of buttoned carriage-cloth
Until the next town, new and nondescript,
Approached with acres of dismantled cars.

At first I didn't notice what a noise
  The weddings made
Each station that we stopped at: sun destroys
The interest of what's happening in the shade,
And down the long cool platforms whoops and skirls
I took for porters larking with the mails,
And went on reading. Once we started, though,
We passed them, grinning and pomaded, girls
In parodies of fashion, heels and veils,
All posed irresolutely, watching us go,

As if out on the end of an event
   Waving goodbye
To something that survived it. Struck, I leant
More promptly out next time, more curiously,
And saw it all again in different terms:
The fathers with broad belts under their suits
And seamy foreheads; mothers loud and fat;
An uncle shouting smut; and then the perms,
The nylon gloves and jewellery-substitutes,
The lemons, mauves, and olive-ochres that

Marked off the girls unreally from the rest.
   Yes, from cafés
And banquet-halls up yards, and bunting-dressed
Coach-party annexes, the wedding-days
Were coming to an end. All down the line
Fresh couples climbed aboard: the rest stood round;
The last confetti and advice were thrown,
And, as we moved, each face seemed to define
Just what it saw departing: children frowned
At something dull; fathers had never known

Success so huge and wholly farcical;
   The women shared
The secret like a happy funeral;
While girls, gripping their handbags tighter, stared
At a religious wounding. Free at last,
And loaded with the sum of all they saw,
We hurried towards London, shuffling gouts of steam.
Now fields were building-plots, and poplars cast
Long shadows over major roads, and for
Some fifty minutes, that in time would seem

Just long enough to settle hats and say
I nearly died,
A dozen marriages got under way.
They watched the landscape, sitting side by side
– An Odeon went past, a cooling tower,
And someone running up to bowl – and none
Thought of the others they would never meet
Or how their lives would contain this hour.
I thought of London spread out in the sun,
Its postal districts packed like squares of wheat:

There we were aimed. And as we raced across
    Bright knots of rail
Past standing Pullmans, walls of blackened moss
Came close, and it was nearly done, this frail
Travelling coincidence; and what it held
Stood ready to be loosed with all the power
That being changed can give. We slowed again,
And as the tightened brakes took hold, there swelled
A sense of falling, like an arrow-shower
Sent out of sight, somewhere becoming rain.

OSCAR WILDE 1854–1900

From THE BALLAD OF READING GAOL

He did not wear his scarlet coat,
For blood and wine are red,
And blood and wine were on his hands
    When they found him with the dead,
The poor dead woman whom he loved,
    And murdered in her bed.

He walked amongst the Trial Men
    In a suit of shabby grey;
A cricket cap was on his head,
    And his step seemed light and gay;
But I never saw a man who looked
  So wistfully at the day.

I never saw a man who looked
    With such a wistful eye
Upon that little tent of blue
    Which prisoners call the sky,
And at every drifting cloud that went
    With sails of silver by.

I walked, with other souls in pain,
    Within another ring,
And was wondering if the man had done
    A great or little thing,
When a voice behind me whispered low,
    'That fellow's got to swing.'

* * * * * *

Six weeks our guardsman walked the yard,
    In the suit of shabby grey:
His cricket cap was on his head,
    And his step seemed light and gay,
But I never saw a man who looked
  So wistfully at the day.

I never saw a man who looked
        With such a wistful eye
Upon that little tent of blue
        Which prisoners call the sky,
And at every wandering cloud that trailed
        Its ravelled fleeces by.

He did not wring his hands, as do
        Those witless men who dare
To try to rear the changeling Hope
        In the cave of black Despair:
He only looked upon the sun,
        And drank the morning air.

He did not wring his hands nor weep,
        Nor did he peek or pine,
But he drank the air as though it held
        Some healthful anodyne;
With open mouth he drank the sun
        As though it had been wine!

And I and all the souls in pain,
        Who tramped the other ring,
Forgot if we ourselves had done
        A great or little thing,
And watched with gaze of dull amaze
        The man who had to swing.

And strange it was to see him pass
        With a step so light and gay,
And strange it was to see him look
        So wistfully at the day,
And strange it was to think that he
        Had such a debt to pay.

                ****

For oak and elm have pleasant leaves
        That in the spring-time shoot:
But grim to see is the gallows-tree,
        With its adder-bitten root,
And, green or dry, a man must die
        Before it bears its fruit!

The loftiest place is that seat of grace
    For which all worldlings try:
But who would stand in hempen band
    Upon a scaffold high,
And through a murderer's collar take
    His last look at the sky?

It is sweet to dance to violins
    When Love and Life are fair:
To dance to flutes, to dance to lutes
    Is delicate and rare:
But it is not sweet with nimble feet
    To dance upon the air!

So with curious eyes and sick surmise
    We watched him day by day,
And wondered if each one of us
    Would end the self-same way,
For none can tell to what red Hell
    His sightless soul may stray.

At last the dead man walked no more
    Amongst the Trial Men,
And I knew that he was standing up
    In the black dock's dreadful pen,
And that never would I see his face
    In God's sweet world again.

Like two doomed ships that pass in storm
    We had crossed each other's way:
But we made no sign, we said no word,
    We had no word to say;
For we did not meet in the holy night,
    But in the shameful day.

A prison wall was round us both,
    Two outcast men we were:
The world had thrust us from its heart,
    And God from out His care:
And the iron gin that waits for Sin
    Had caught us in its snare.

****

In Debtors' Yard the stones are hard,
    And the dripping wall is high,
So it was there he took the air
    Beneath the leaden sky,
And by each side a Warder walked,
    For fear the man might die.

Or else he sat with those who watched
    His anguish night and day;
Who watched him when he rose to weep,
    And when he crouched to pray;
Who watched him lest himself should rob
    Their scaffold of its prey.

****

And twice a day he smoked his pipe,
    And drank his quart of beer:
His soul was resolute, and held
    No hiding-place for fear;
He often said that he was glad
    The hangman's hands were near.

But why he said so strange a thing
    No Warder dared to ask:
For he to whom a watcher's doom
    Is given as his task,
Must set a lock upon his lips,
    And make his face a mask.

Or else he might be moved, and try
    To comfort or console:
And what should Human Pity do
    Pent up in Murderers' Hole?
What word of grace in such a place
    Could help a brother's soul?

****

We tore the tarry rope to shreds
    With blunt and bleeding nails;
We rubbed the doors, and scrubbed the floors,
    And cleaned the shining rails:

And, rank by rank, we soaped the plank,
    And clattered with the pails.

We sewed the sacks, we broke the stones,
    We turned the dusty drill:
We banged the tins, and bawled the hymns,
    And sweated on the mill:
But in the heart of every man
    Terror was lying still.

So still it lay that every day
    Crawled like a weed-clogged wave:
And we forgot the bitter lot
    That waits for fool and knave,
Till once, as we tramped in from work,
    We passed an open grave.

With yawning mouth the yellow hole
    Gaped for a living thing;
The very mud cried out for blood
    To the thirsty asphalte ring:
And we knew that ere one dawn grew fair
    Some prisoner had to swing.

Right in we went, with soul intent
    On Death and Dread and Doom:
The hangman, with his little bag,
    Went shuffling through the gloom:
And each man trembled as he crept
    Into his numbered tomb.

* * * * * * *

That night the empty corridors
    Were full of forms of Fear,
And up and down the iron town
    Stole feet we could not hear,
And through the bars that hide the stars
    White faces seemed to peer.

He lay as one who lies and dreams
    In a pleasant meadow-land,
The watchers watched him as he slept,

And could not understand
How one could sleep so sweet a sleep
With a hangman close at hand.

But there is no sleep when men must weep
Who never yet have wept:
So we – the fool, the fraud, the knave –
That endless vigil kept,
And through each brain on hands of pain
Another's terror crept.

****

There is no chapel on the day
On which they hang a man:
The Chaplain's heart is far too sick,
Or his face is far too wan,
Or there is that written in his eyes
Which none should look upon.

So they kept us close till nigh on noon,
And then they rang the bell,
And the Warders with their jingling keys
Opened each listening cell,
And down the iron stair we tramped,
Each from his separate Hell.

Out into God's sweet air we went,
But not in wonted way,
For this man's face was white with fear,
And that man's face was gray,
And I never saw sad men who looked
So wistfully at the day.

I never saw sad men who looked
With such a wistful eye
Upon that little tent of blue
We prisoners call the sky,
And at every careless cloud that passed
In happy freedom by.

The Warders strutted up and down,
And kept their herd of brutes,

Their uniforms were spick and span,
        And they wore their Sunday suits,
But we knew the work they had been at,
        By the quicklime on their boots.

For where a grave had opened wide,
        There was no grave at all:
Only a stretch of mud and sand
        By the hideous prison-wall,
And a little heap of burning lime,
        That the man should have his pall.

For three long years they will not sow
        Or root or seedling there:
For three long years the unblessed spot
        Will sterile be and bare,
And look upon the wondering sky
        With unreproachful stare.

They think a murderer's heart would taint
        Each simple seed they sow.
It is not true! God's kindly earth
        Is kindlier than men know,
And the red rose would but blow more red,
        The white rose whiter blow.

THOMAS HOOD 1799-1845

I REMEMBER, I REMEMBER

I remember, I remember,
  The house where I was born,
The little window where the sun
  Came peeping in at morn;
He never came a wink too soon,
  Nor brought too long a day,
But now, I often wish the night
  Had borne my breath away.

I remember, I remember,
  The roses, red and white;
The violets, and the lily-cups,
  Those flowers made of light!
The lilacs where the robin built,
  And where my brother set
The laburnum on his birthday –
  The tree is living yet!

I remember, I remember,
  Where I was used to swing;
And thought the air must rush as fresh
  To swallows on the wing:
My spirit flew in feathers then,
  That is so heavy now,
And summer pools could hardly cool
  The fever on my brow!

I remember, I remember,
  The fir trees dark and high;
I used to think their slender tops
  Were close against the sky:
It was a childish ignorance,
  But now 'tis little joy
To know I'm farther off from Heav'n
  Than when I was a boy.

PHILIP LARKIN 1922–80

THIS BE THE VERSE

They fuck you up, your mum and dad.
   They may not mean to, but they do.
They fill you with the faults they had
   And add some extra, just for you.

But they were fucked up in their turn
   By fools in old-style hats and coats,
Who half the time were soppy-stern
   And half at one another's throats.

Man hands on misery to man.
   It deepens like a coastal shelf.
Get out as early as you can,
   And don't have any kids yourself.

57

D.H. LAWRENCE 1885-1930

SNAKE

A snake came to my water-trough
On a hot, hot day, and I in pyjamas for the heat,
To drink there.

In the deep, strange-scented shade of the great dark carob-tree
I came down the steps with my pitcher
And must wait, must stand and wait, for there he was at the trough
· before me.

He reached down from a fissure in the earth-wall in the gloom
And trailed his yellow-brown slackness soft-bellied down, over the
    edge of the stone trough
And rested his throat upon the stone bottom,
And where the water had dripped from the tap, in a small clearness,
He sipped with his straight mouth,
Softly drank through his straight gums, into his slack long body,
Silently.

Someone was before me at my water trough,
And I, like a second comer, waiting.

He lifted his head from his drinking, as cattle do,
And looked at me vaguely, as drinking cattle do,
And flickered his two-forked tongue from his lips, and mused a
    moment,
And stooped and drank a little more,
Being earth-brown, earth-golden from the burning bowels of the
    earth
On the day of Sicilian July, with Etna smoking.

The voice of my education said to me
He must be killed,
For in Sicily the black, black snakes are innocent, the gold are
    venomous.

And voices in me said, If you were a man
You would take a stick and break him now, and finish him off.
But must I confess how I liked him,

95

How glad I was he had come like a guest in quiet, to drink at my
     water-trough
And depart peaceful, pacified, and thankless,
Into the burning bowels of this earth?

Was it cowardice, that I dared not kill him?
Was it perversity, that I longed to talk to him?
Was it humility, to feel so honoured?
I felt so honoured.

And yet those voices:
If you were not afraid, you would kill him!

And truly I was afraid, I was most afraid,
But even so, honoured still more
That he should seek my hospitality
From out the dark door of the secret earth.

He drank enough
And lifted his head, dreamily, as one who has drunken,
And flickered his tongue like a forked night on the air, so black,
Seeming to lick his lips,
And looked around like a god, unseeing, into the air,
And slowly turned his head,
And slowly, very slowly, as if thrice adream,
Proceeded to draw his slow length curving round
And climb again the broken bank of my wall-face.

And as he put his head into that dreadful hole,
And as he slowly drew up, snake-easing his shoulders, and
     entered farther,
A sort of horror, a sort of protest against his withdrawing into
     that horrid black hole,
Deliberately going into the blackness, and slowly drawing
     himself after,
Overcame me now his back was turned.

I looked round, I put down my pitcher,
I picked up a clumsy log
And threw it at the water trough with a clatter.

I think it did not hit him,
But suddenly that part of him that was left behind convulsed
    in undignified haste,
Writhed like lightning, and was gone
Into the black hole, the earth-lipped fissure in the wall-front,
At which, in the intense still noon, I stared with fascination.

And immediately I regretted it.
I thought how paltry, how vulgar, what a mean act!
I despised myself and the voices of my accursed human
    education.

And I thought of the albatross,
And I wished he would come back, my snake.

For he seemed to me again like a king,
Like a king in exile, uncrowned in the underworld,
Now due to be crowned again.

And so, I missed my chance with one of the lords
Of life.
And I have something to expiate;
A pettiness.

RUPERT BROOKE 1887–1915

THE GREAT LOVER

I have been so great a lover: filled my days
So proudly with the splendour of Love's praise,
The pain, the calm, and the astonishment,
Desire illimitable, and still content,
And all dear names men use, to cheat despair,
For the perplexed and viewless streams that bear
Our hearts at random down the dark of life.
Now, ere the unthinking silence on that strife
Steals down, I would cheat drowsy Death so far,
My night shall be remembered for a star
That outshone all the suns of all men's days.
Shall I not crown them with immortal praise
Whom I have loved, who have given me, dared with me
High secrets, and in darkness knelt to see
The inenarrable godhead of delight?
Love is a flame: – we have beaconed the world's night,
A city: – and we have built it, these and I.
An emperor: – we have taught the world to die.
So, for their sakes I loved, ere I go hence,
And the high cause of Love's magnificence,
And to keep loyalties young, I'll write those names
Golden for ever, eagles, crying flames,
And set them as a banner, that men may know,
To dare the generations, burn, and blow
Out on the wind of Time, shining and streaming. . . .

These I have loved:
          White plates and cups, clean-gleaming,
Ringed with blue lines; and feathery, faery dust;
Wet roofs, beneath the lamp-light: the strong crust
Of friendly bread; and many-tasting food;
Rainbows; and the blue bitter smoke of wood;
And radiant raindrops couching in cool flowers;
And flowers themselves, that sway through sunny hours,
Dreaming of moths that drink them under the moon;
Then, the cool kindliness of sheets, that soon
Smooth away trouble; and the rough male kiss

Of blankets; grainy wood; live hair that is
Shining and free; blue-massing clouds; the keen
Unpassioned beauty of a great machine;
The benison of hot water; furs to touch;
The good smell of old clothes; and other such –
The comfortable smell of friendly fingers,
Hair's fragrance, and the musty reek that lingers
About dead leaves and last year's ferns. . . .
                              Dear names,
And thousand other throng to me! Royal flames;
Sweet water's dimpling laugh from tap or spring;
Holes in the ground; and voices that do sing;
Voices in laughter, too; and body's pain,
Soon turned to peace; and the deep-panting train;
Firm sands; the little dulling edge of foam
That browns and dwindles as the wave goes home;
And washen stones, gay for an hour; the cold
Graveness of iron; moist black earthen mould;
Sleep; and high places; footprints in the dew;
And oaks; and brown horse-chestnuts, glossy-new;
And new-peeled sticks; and shining pools on grass;-
All these have been my loves. And these shall pass.
Whatever passes not, in the great hour,
Nor all my passion, all my prayers, have power
To hold them with me through the gate of Death.
They'll play deserter, turn with the traitor breath,
Break the high bond we made, and sell Love's trust
And sacramented covenant to the dust.
——Oh, never a doubt but, somewhere, I shall wake,
And give what's left of love again, and make
New friends, now strangers. . . .
                              But the best I've known
Stays here, and changes, breaks, grows old, is blown
About the winds of the world, and fades from brains
Of living men, and dies.
                              Nothing remains.

O dear my loves, O faithless, once again
This one last gift I give: that after men
Shall know, and later lovers, far-removed,
Praise you, 'All these were lovely'; say, 'He loved.'

Mataiea, 1914

99

ROBERT BURNS 1759–1796

A RED, RED ROSE

TUNE: MAJOR GRAHAM

O my luve's like a red, red rose,
  That's newly sprung in June;
O my luve's like the melodie
  That's sweetly play'd in tune.

As fair art thou, my bonie lass,
  So deep in luve am I,
And I will luve thee still, my Dear,
  Till a' the seas gang dry.

Till a' the seas gang dry, my Dear,
  And the rocks melt wi' the sun:
I will luve thee still, my Dear,
  While the sands o' life shall run.

And fare thee weel, my only Luve,
  And fare thee weel a while!
And I will come again, my Luve,
  Tho' it were ten thousand mile!

LOUIS MACNEICE 1907-63

THE SUNLIGHT ON THE GARDEN

The sunlight on the garden
Hardens and grows cold,
We cannot cage the minute
Within its nets of gold,
When all is told
We cannot beg for pardon.

Our freedom as free lances
Advances towards its end;
The earth compels, upon it
Sonnets and birds descend;
And soon, my friend,
We shall have no time for dances.

The sky was good for flying
Defying the church bells
And every evil iron
Siren and what it tells:
The earth compels,
We are dying, Egypt, dying

And not expecting pardon,
Hardened in heart anew,
But glad to have sat under
Thunder and rain with you,
And grateful too
For sunlight on the garden.

RUPERT BROOKE 1887–1915

THE OLD VICARAGE, GRANTCHESTER

(*Café des Westens, Berlin, May 1912*)

Just now the lilac is in bloom,
All before my little room;
And in my flower-beds, I think,
Smile the carnation and the pink;
And down the borders, well I know,
The poppy and the pansy blow –
Oh! there the chestnuts, summer through,
Beside the river make for you
A tunnel of green gloom, and sleep
Deeply above; and green and deep
The stream mysterious glides beneath,
Green as a dream and deep as death.
– Oh, damn! I know it! and I know
How the May fields all golden show,
And when the day is young and sweet,
Gild gloriously the bare feet.
That run to bathe –
                    Du lieber Gott!

Here am I, sweating, sick, and hot,
And there the shadowed waters fresh
Lean up to embrace the naked flesh.
Temperamentvoll German Jews
Drink beer around – and *there* the dews
Are soft beneath a morn of gold.
Here tulips bloom as they are told;
Unkempt about those hedges blows
An English unofficial rose;
And there the unregulated sun
Slopes down to rest when day is done,
And wakes a vague unpunctual star,
A slippered Hesper; and there are
Meads towards Haslingfield and Coton
Where *das Betreten*'s not *verboten.*

Ειυε γεψοιμηψ... would I were
In Grantchester, in Grantchester!
Some, it may be, can get in touch
With Nature there, or Earth, or such.
And clever modern men have seen
A Faun a-peeping through the green,
And felt the Classics were not dead,
To glimpse a Naiad's reedy head,
Or hear the Goat-foot piping low: –
But these are things I do not know.
I only know that you may lie
Day-long and watch the Cambridge sky,
And, flower-lulled in sleepy grass,
Hear the cool lapse of hours pass,
Until the centuries blend and blur
In Grantchester, in Grantchester –
Still in the dawnlit waters cool
His ghostly Lordship swims his pool,
And tries the strokes, essays the tricks,
Long learnt on Hellespont, or Styx.
Dan Chaucer hears his river still
Chatter beneath a phantom mill.

Tennyson notes, with studious eye,
How Cambridge waters hurry by –
And in that garden, black and white,
Creep whispers through the grass all night;
And spectral dance, before the dawn,
A hundred Vicars down the lawn;
Curates, long dust, will come and go
On lissom, clerical, printless toe;
And oft between the boughs is seen
The sly shade of a Rural Dean –
Till, at a shiver in the skies,
Vanishing with Satanic cries,

The prim ecclesiastic rout
Leaves but a startled sleeper-out,
Grey heavens, the first bird's drowsy calls,
The falling house that never falls.

God! I will pack, and take a train,
And get me to England once again!
For England's the one land, I know,
Where men with Splendid Hearts may go;
And Cambridgeshire, of all England,
The shire for Men who Understand;
And of *that* district I prefer
The lovely hamlet Grantchester.
For Cambridge people rarely smile,
Being urban, squat, and packed with guile;
And Royston men in the far South
Are black and fierce and strange of mouth;
At Over they fling oaths at one,
And worse than oaths at Trumpington,
And Ditton girls are mean and dirty,
And there's none in Harston under thirty,
And folks in Shelford and those parts
Have twisted lips and twisted hearts,
And Barton men make Cockney rhymes,
And Coton's full of nameless crimes,
And things are done you'd not believe
At Madingley, on Christmas Eve.
Strong men have run for miles and miles,
When one from Cherry Hinton smiles;
Strong men have blanched, and shot their wives,
Rather than send them to St Ives;
Strong men have cried like babes, bydam,
To hear what happened at Babraham.
But Grantchester! ah, Grantchester!
There's peace and holy quiet there,
Great clouds along pacific skies,
And men and women with straight eyes,
Lithe children lovelier than a dream,
A bosky wood, a slumbrous stream,
And little kindly winds that creep

Round twilight corners, half asleep.
In Grantchester their skins are white;
They bathe by day, they bathe by night;
The women there do all they ought;
The men observe the Rules of Thought.
They love the Good; they worship Truth;
They laugh uproariously in youth;
(And when they get to feeling old,
They up and shoot themselves, I'm told) –

Ah God! to see the branches stir
Across the moon at Grantchester!
To smell the thrilling-sweet and rotten
Unforgettable, unforgotten
River-smell, and hear the breeze
Sobbing in the little trees.
Say, do the elm-clumps greatly stand
Still guardians of that holy land?
The chestnuts shade, in reverend dream,
The yet unacademic stream?
Is dawn a secret shy and cold
Anadyomene, silver-gold?
And sunset still a golden sea
From Haslingfield to Madingley?

And after, ere the night is born,
Do hares come out about the corn?
Oh, is the water sweet and cool,
Gentle and brown, above the pool?
And laughs the immortal river still
Under the mill, under the mill?
Say, is there Beauty yet to find?
And Certainty? and Quiet kind?
Deep meadows yet, for to forget
The lies, and truths, and pain? – oh! yet
Stands the Church clock at ten to three?
And is there honey still for tea?

JOHN BETJEMAN 1906–84

DIARY OF A CHURCH MOUSE

Here among long-discarded cassocks,
Damp stools, and half-split open hassocks,
Here where the Vicar never looks
I nibble through old service books.
Lean and alone I spend my days
Behind this Church of England baize.
I share my dark forgotten room
With two oil-lamps and half a broom.
The cleaner never bothers me,
So here I eat my frugal tea.
My bread is sawdust mixed with straw;
My jam is polish for the floor.

    Christmas and Easter may be feasts
For congregations and for priests,
And so may Whitsun. All the same,
They do not fill my meagre frame.
For me the only feast at all
Is Autumn's Harvest Festival,
When I can satisfy my want
With ears of corn around the font.
I climb the eagle's brazen head
To burrow through a loaf of bread.
I scramble up the pulpit stair
And gnaw the marrows hanging there.

    It is enjoyable to taste
These items ere they go to waste,
But how annoying when one finds
That other mice with pagan minds
Come into church my food to share
Who have no proper business there.
Two field mice who have no desire
To be baptized, invade the choir.
A large and most unfriendly rat
Comes in to see what we are at.
He says he thinks there is no God

And yet he comes ... it's rather odd.
This year he stole a sheaf of wheat
(It screened our special preacher's seat),
And prosperous mice from fields away
Come in to hear the organ play,
And under cover of its notes
Eat through the altar's sheaf of oats.
A Low Church mouse, who thinks that I
Am too papistical, and High,
Yet somehow doesn't think it wrong
To munch through Harvest Evensong,
While I, who starve the whole year through,
Must share my food with rodents who
Except at this time of the year
Not once inside the church appear.
     Within the human world I know
Such goings-on could not be so,
For human beings only do
What their religion tells them to.
They read the Bible every day
And always, night and morning, pray,
And just like me, the good church mouse,
Worship each week in God's own house,
     But all the same it's strange to me
How very full the church can be
With people I don't see at all
Except at Harvest Festival.

WALTER DE LA MARE 1873–1956

SILVER

Slowly, silently, now the moon
Walks the night in her silver shoon;
This way, and that, she peers, and sees
Silver fruit upon silver trees;
One by one the casements catch
Her beams beneath the silvery thatch;
Couched in his kennel, like a log,
With paws of silver sleeps the dog;
From their shadowy cote the white breasts peep
Of doves in a silver-feathered sleep;
A harvest mouse goes scampering by,
With silver claws, and silver eye;
And moveless fish in the water gleam,
By silver reeds in a silver stream.

GERARD MANLEY HOPKINS 1844–89

PIED BEAUTY

Glory be to God for dappled things –
  For skies of couple-colour as a brinded cow;
    For rose-moles all in stipple upon trout that swim;
Fresh-firecoal chestnut-falls; finches' wings;
  Landscape plotted and pieced – fold, fallow, and plough;
    And áll trádes, their gear and tackle and trim.

All things counter, original, spare, strange;
  Whatever is fickle, freckled (who knows how?)
    With swift, slow; sweet, sour; adazzle, dim;
He fathers-forth whose beauty is past change:
      Praise him.

65

LOUIS MACNEICE 1907–63

PRAYER BEFORE BIRTH

I am not yet born; O hear me.
Let not the bloodsucking bat or the rat or the stoat or the
    club-footed ghoul come near me.

I am not yet born, console me.
I fear that the human race may with tall walls wall me,
    with strong drugs dope me, with wise lies lure me,
        on black racks rack me, in blood-baths roll me.

I am not yet born; provide me
With water to dandle me, grass to grow for me, trees to talk
    to me, sky to sing to me, birds and a white light
        in the back of my mind to guide me.

I am not yet born; forgive me
For the sins that in me the world shall commit, my words
    when they speak me, my thoughts when they think me,
        my treason engendered by traitors beyond me,
            my life when they murder by means of my
                hands, my death when they live me.

I am not yet born; rehearse me
In the parts I must play and the cues I must take when
    old men lecture me, bureaucrats hector me, mountains
        frown at me, lovers laugh at me, the white
            waves call me to folly and the desert calls
                me to doom and the beggar refuses
                    my gift and my children curse me.

I am not yet born; O hear me,
Let not the man who is beast or who thinks he is God
    come near me.

I am not yet born; O fill me
With strength against those who would freeze my
    humanity, would dragoon me into a lethal automaton,
    would make me a cog in a machine, a thing with
    one face, a thing, and against all those
    who would dissipate my entirety, would
    blow me like thistledown hither and
        thither or hither and thither
        like water held in the
        hands would spill me.

Let them not make me a stone and let them not spill me.
Otherwise kill me.

T.S.ELIOT 1885–1965

MACAVITY: THE MYSTERY CAT

Macavity's a Mystery Cat: he's called the Hidden Paw –
For he's the master criminal who can defy the Law.
He's the bafflement of Scotland Yard, the Flying Squad's despair:
For when they reach the scene of crime – *Macavity's not there!*

Macavity, Macavity, there's no one like Macavity,
He's broken every human law, he breaks the law of gravity.
His powers of levitation would make a fakir stare,
And when you reach the scene of crime – *Macavity's not there!*
You may seek him in the basement, you may look up in the air –
But I tell you once and once again, *Macavity's not there!*

Macavity's a ginger cat, he's very tall and thin;
You would know him if you saw him, for his eyes are sunken in.
His brow is deeply lined with thought, his head is highly domed;
His coat is dusty from neglect, his whiskers are uncombed.
He sways his head from side to side, with movements like a snake;
And when you think he's half asleep, he's always wide awake.

Macavity, Macavity, there's no one like Macavity,
For he's a fiend in feline shape, a monster of depravity.
You may meet him in a by-street, you may see him in the square –
But when a crime's discovered, then *Macavity's not there!*

He's outwardly respectable. (They say he cheats at cards.)
And his footprints are not found in any file of Scotland Yard's.
And when the larder's looted, or the jewel-case is rifled,
Or when the milk is missing, or another Peke's been stifled,
Or the greenhouse glass is broken, and the trellis past repair –
Ay, there's the wonder of the thing! *Macavity's not there!*

And when the Foreign Office find a Treaty's gone astray,
Or the Admiralty lose some plans and drawings by the way,
There may be a scrap of paper in the hall or on the stair –
But it's useless to investigate – *Macavity's not there!*
And when the loss has been disclosed, the Secret Service say:
'It *must* have been Macavity!' – but he's a mile away.
You'll be sure to find him resting, or a-licking of his thumbs,
Or engaged in doing complicated long division sums.

Macavity, Macavity, there's no one like Macavity,
There never was a Cat of such deceitfulness and suavity.
He always has an alibi, and one or two to spare:
At whatever time the deed took place – MACAVITY WASN'T THERE!
And they say that all the Cats whose wicked deeds are widely known
(I might mention Mungojerrie, I might mention Griddlebone)
Are nothing more than agents for the Cat who all the time
Just controls their operations: the Napoleon of Crime!

THOMAS HARDY 1840–1928

AFTERWARDS

When the Present has latched its postern behind my tremulous stay,
    And the May month flaps its glad green leaves like wings,
Delicate-filmed as new-spun silk, will the neighbours say
    'He was a man who used to notice such things'?

If it be in the dusk when, like an eyelid's soundless blink,
    The dewfall-hawk comes crossing the shades to alight
Upon the wind-warped upland thorn, a gazer may think,
    'To him this must have been a familiar sight'.

If I pass during some nocturnal blackness, mothy and warm,
    When the hedgehog travels furtively over the lawn,
One may say, 'He strove that such innocent creatures should come to
        no harm,
    But he could do little for them; and now he is gone'.

If, when hearing that I have been stilled at last, they stand at the door,
    Watching the full-starred heavens that winter sees,
Will this thought rise on those who will meet my face no more,
    'He was one who had an eye for such mysteries'?

And will any say when my bell of quittance is heard in the gloom,
    And a crossing breeze cuts a pause in its outrollings,
Till they rise again, as they were a new bell's boom,
    'He hears it not now, but used to notice such things'?

G.K. CHESTERTON 1874–1936

THE DONKEY

When fishes flew and forests walked
And figs grew upon thorn,
Some moment when the moon was blood
Then surely I was born.

With monstrous head and sickening cry
And ears like errant wings,
The devil's walking parody
On all four-footed things.

The tattered outlaw of the earth,
Of ancient crooked will;
Starve, scourge, deride me: I am dumb,
I keep my secret still.

Fools! For I also had my hour;
One far fierce hour and sweet:
There was a shout about my ears,
And palms before my feet.

ROBERT BROWNING 1812–1889

MY LAST DUCHESS

That's my last Duchess painted on the wall,
Looking as if she were alive. I call
That piece a wonder, now: Frà Pandolf's hands
Worked busily a day, and there she stands.
Will't please you sit and look at her? I said
Frà Pandolf by design, for never read
Strangers like you that pictured countenance,
The depth and passion of its earnest glance,
But to myself they turned (since none puts by
The curtain I have drawn for you, but I)
And seemed as they would ask me, if they durst,
How such a glance came there; so, not the first
Are you to turn and ask thus. Sir, 'twas not
Her husband's presence only, called that spot
Of joy into the Duchess' cheek: perhaps
Frà Pandolf chanced to say 'Her mantle laps
Over my lady's wrist too much,' or 'Paint
Must never hope to reproduce the faint
Half-flush that dies along her throat': such stuff
Was courtesy, she thought, and cause enough
For calling up that spot of joy. She had
A heart – how shall I say? – too soon made glad,
Too easily impressed; she liked whate'er
She looked on, and her looks went everywhere.
Sir, 'twas all one! My favour at her breast,
The dropping of the daylight in the West,
The bough of cherries some officious fool
Broke in the orchard for her, the white mule
She rode with round the terrace – all and each
Would draw from her alike the approving speech,
Or blush, at least. She thanked men, – good! but thanked
Somehow – I know not how – as if she ranked
My gift of a nine-hundred-years-old name
With anybody's gift. Who'd stoop to blame
This sort of trifling? Even had you skill

In speech – (which I have not) – to make your will
Quite clear to such an one, and say, 'Just this
Or that in you disgusts me; here you miss,
Or there exceed the mark' – and if she let
Herself be lessoned so, nor plainly set
Her wits to yours, forsooth, and made excuse,
– E'en then would be some stooping; and I choose
Never to stoop. Oh sir, she smiled, no doubt
Whene'er I passed her; but who passed without
Much the same smile? This grew; I gave commands;
Then all smiles stopped together. There she stands
As if alive. Will't please you rise? We'll meet
The company below, then. I repeat,
The Count your master's known munificence
Is ample warrant that no just pretence
Of mine for dowry will be disallowed;
Though his fair daughter's self, as I avowed
At starting, is my object. Nay, we'll go
Together down, sir. Notice Neptune, though,
Taming a sea-horse, thought a rarity,
Which Claus of Innsbruck cast in bronze for me!

JOHN BETJEMAN 1906–84

CHRISTMAS

The bells of waiting Advent ring,
   The Tortoise stove is lit again
And lamp-oil light across the night
   Has caught the streaks of winter rain
In many a stained-glass window sheen
From Crimson Lake to Hooker's Green.

The holly in the windy hedge
   And round the Manor House the yew
Will soon be stripped to deck the ledge,
   The altar, font and arch and pew,
So that the villagers can say
'The church looks nice' on Christmas Day.

Provincial public houses blaze
   And Corporation tramcars clang,
On lighted tenements I gaze
   Where paper decorations hang,
And bunting in the red Town Hall
Says 'Merry Christmas to you all'.

And London shops on Christmas Eve
   Are strung with silver bells and flowers
As hurrying clerks the City leave
   To pigeon-haunted classic towers,
And marbled clouds go scudding by
The many-steepled London sky.

And girls in slacks remember Dad,
   And oafish louts remember Mum,
And sleepless children's hearts are glad,
   And Christmas-morning bells say 'Come!'
Even to shining ones who dwell
Safe in the Dorchester Hotel.

And is it true? And is it true,
This most tremendous tale of all,
Seen in a stained-glass window's hue,
A Baby in an ox's stall?
The Maker of the stars and sea
Become a Child on earth for me?

And is it true? For if it is,
No loving fingers tying strings
Around those tissued fripperies,
The sweet and silly Christmas things,
Bath salts and inexpensive scent
And hideous tie so kindly meant,

No love that in a family dwells,
No carolling in frosty air,
Nor all the steeple-shaking bells
Can with this single Truth compare –
That God was Man in Palestine
And lives to-day in Bread and Wine.

TED HUGHES 1930–

THE THOUGHT-FOX

I imagine this midnight moment's forest:
Something else is alive
Beside the clock's loneliness
And this blank page where my fingers move.

Through the window I see no star:
Something more near
Though deeper within darkness
Is entering the loneliness:

Cold, delicately as the dark snow
A fox's nose touches twig, leaf;
Two eyes serve a movement, that now
And again now, and now, and now

Sets neat prints into the snow
Between trees, and warily a lame
Shadow lags by stump and in hollow
Of a body that is bold to come

Across clearings, an eye,
A widening deepening greenness,
Brilliantly, concentratedly,
Coming about its own business

Till with a sudden sharp hot stink of fox
It enters the dark hole of the head.
The window is starless still; the clock ticks,
The page is printed.

T.S. ELIOT 1885–1965

PRELUDES

I

The winter evening settles down
With smell of steaks in passageways.
Six o'clock.
The burnt-out ends of smoky days.

And now a gusty shower wraps
The grimy scraps
Of withered leaves about your feet
And newspapers from vacant lots;
The showers beat
On broken blinds and chimney-pots,
And at the corner of the street
A lonely cab-horse steams and stamps.

And then the lighting of the lamps.

II

The morning comes to consciousness
Of faint stale smells of beer
From the sawdust-trampled street
With all its muddy feet that press
To early coffee-stands.

With the other masquerades
That time resumes,
One thinks of all the hands
That are raising dingy shades
In a thousand furnished rooms.

III

You tossed a blanket from the bed,
You lay upon your back, and waited;
You dozed, and watched the night revealing
The thousand sordid images
Of which your soul was constituted;
They flickered against the ceiling.
And when all the world came back

And the light crept up between the shutters,
And you heard the sparrows in the gutters,
You had such a vision of the street
As the street hardly understands;
Sitting along the bed's edge, where
You curled the papers from your hair,
Or clasped the yellow soles of feet
In the palms of both soiled hands.

I V

His soul stretched tight across the skies
That fade behind a city block,
Or trampled by insistent feet
At four and five and six o'clock;
And short square fingers stuffing pipes,
And evening newspapers, and eyes
Assured of certain certainties,
The conscience of a blackened street
Impatient to assume the world.

I am moved by fancies that are curled
Around these images, and cling:
The notion of some infinitely gentle
Infinitely suffering thing.

Wipe your hand across your mouth, and laugh;
The worlds revolve like ancient women
Gathering fuel in vacant lots.

GEORGE HERBERT 1593–1633

LOVE (III)

Love bade me welcome; yet my soul drew back,
    Guilty of dust and sin.
But quick-eyed Love, observing me grow slack
    From my first entrance in,
Drew nearer to me, sweetly questioning
    If I lack'd anything.

'A guest,' I answer'd, 'worthy to be here:'
    Love said, 'You shall be he.'
'I, the unkind, ungrateful? Ah, my dear,
    I cannot look on thee.'
Love took my hand and smiling did reply,
    'Who made the eyes but I?'

'Truth, Lord, but I have marr'd them: let my shame
    Go where it doth deserve.'
'And know you not,' says Love, 'Who bore the blame?'
    'My dear, then I will serve.'
'You must sit down,' says Love, 'and taste my meat.'
    So I did sit and eat.

ALFRED, LORD TENNYSON 1809–92

THE CHARGE OF THE LIGHT BRIGADE

I

Half a league, half a league,
　Half a league onward,
All in the valley of Death
　Rode the six hundred.
'Forward, the Light Brigade!
Charge for the guns!' he said;
Into the valley of Death
　Rode the six hundred.

II

'Forward, the Light Brigade!'
Was there a man dismay'd?
Not tho' the soldier knew
　Some one had blunder'd:
Their's not to make reply,
Their's not to reason why,
Their's but to do and die:
Into the valley of Death
　Rode the six hundred.

III

Cannon to right of them,
Cannon to left of them,
Cannon in front of them
　Volley'd and thunder'd;
Storm'd at with shot and
shell,
Boldly they rode and well,
Into the jaws of Death,
Into the mouth of Hell
　Rode the six hundred.

IV

Flash'd all their sabres bare,
Flash'd as they turn'd in air,
Sabring the gunners there,
Charging an army, while
   All the world wonder'd:
Plunged in the battery-smoke
Right thro' the line they broke;
Cossack and Russian
Reel'd from the sabre-stroke
   Shatter'd and sunder'd.
Then they rode back, but not,
   Not the six hundred.

V

Cannon to right of them,
Cannon to left of them,
Cannon behind them
   Volley'd and thunder'd;
Storm'd at with shot and shell,
While horse and hero fell,
They that had fought so well
Came thro' the jaws of Death
Back from the mouth of Hell,
All that was left of them,
   Left of six hundred.

VI

When can their glory fade?
O the wild charge they made!
   All the world wonder'd.
Honour the charge they made!
Honour the Light Brigade,
   Noble six hundred!

JOHN CLARE 1793–1864

I AM

I am: yet what I am none cares or knows,
    My friends forsake me like a memory lost;
I am the self-consumer of my woes,
    They rise and vanish in oblivious host,
Like shades in love and death's oblivion lost;
And yet I am, and live with shadows tost

Into the nothingness of scorn and noise,
    Into the living sea of waking dreams,
Where there is neither sense of life nor joys,
    But the vast shipwreck of my life's esteems;
And een the dearest – that I loved the best –
Are strange – nay, rather stranger than the rest.

I long for scenes where man has never trod;
    A place where woman never smiled or wept;
There to abide with my Creator, GOD,
    And sleep as I in childhood sweetly slept:
Untroubling and untroubled where I lie;
The grass below – above the vaulted sky.

FRANCIS THOMPSON 1859–1907

THE HOUND OF HEAVEN

I fled Him, down the nights and down the days;
   I fled Him down the arches of the years;
I fled Him, down the labyrinthine ways
   Of my own mind; and in the mist of tears
I hid from Him, and under running laughter.
     Up vistaed hopes I sped;
     And shot, precipitated.
Adown Titanic glooms of chasmèd fears,
   From those strong Feet that followed, followed after.
     But with unhurrying chase,
     And unperturbed pace,
Deliberate speed, majestic instancy
     They beat – and a Voice beat
     More instant than the Feet –
'All things betray thee, who betrayest Me.'

     I pleaded, outlaw-wise,
By many a hearted casement, curtained red,
   Trellised with intertwining charities;
(For, though I knew His love Who followèd,
     Yet was I sore adread
Lest, having Him, I must have naught beside);
But, if one little casement parted wide,
   The gust of His approach would clash it to.
Fear wist not to evade, as Love wist to pursue.
Across the margent of the world I fled,
   And troubled the gold gateways of the stars,
   Smiting for shelter on their clangèd bars;
     Fretted to dulcet jars
And silvern chatter the pale ports o' the moon.
I said to dawn, Be sudden; to eve, Be soon;
   With thy young skiey blossoms heap me over
   From this tremendous Lover!
Float thy vague veil about me, lest He see!
   I tempted all His servitors, but to find

My own betrayal in their constancy,
In faith to Him their fickleness to me,
   Their traitorous trueness, and their loyal deceit.
To all swift things for swiftness did I sue;
Clung to the whistling mane of every wind.
   But whether, they swept, smoothly fleet,
   The long savannahs of the blue;
      Or whether, Thunder-driven,
   They clanged his chariot 'thwart a heaven
Plashy with flying lightnings round the spurn o' their feet:
   Fear wist not to evade as Love wist to pursue.
      Still with unhurrying chase,
      And unperturbed pace,
Deliberate speed, majestic instancy,
      Came on the following Feet,
      And a Voice above their beat –
'Naught shelters thee, who wilt not shelter Me.'

      Now of that long pursuit
      Comes on at hand the bruit:
That Voice is round me like a bursting sea:
      'And is thy earth so marred,
      Shattered in shard on shard?
Lo, all things fly thee, for thou fliest Me!
   Strange, piteous, futile thing,
Wherefore should any set thee love apart?
Seeing none but I makes much of naught' (He said)
'And human love needs human meriting:
      How hast thou merited –
Of all man's clotted clay the dingiest clot?
      Alack, thou knowest not
How little worthy of any love thou art!
Whom wilt thou find to love ignoble thee
      Save Me, save only Me?
All which I took from thee I did but take,

128

Not for thy harms,
But just that thou might'st seek it in My arms.
All which thy child's mistake
Fancies as lost, I have stored for thee at home:
Rise, clasp My hand, and come!'

Halts by me that footfall:
Is my gloom, after all,
Shade of His hand, outstretched caressingly?
'Ah, fondest, blindest, weakest,
I am He Whom thou seekest!
Thou dravest love from thee, who dravest Me.'

CHRISTOPHER MARLOWE 1564–93

THE PASSIONATE SHEPHERD TO HIS LOVE

Come live with me and be my Love,
And we will all the pleasures prove
That hills and valleys, dale and field,
And all the craggy mountains yield.

There will we sit upon the rocks
And see the shepherds feed their flocks,
By shallow rivers, to whose falls
Melodious birds sing madrigals.

There will I make thee beds of roses
And a thousand fragrant posies,
A cap of flowers, and a kirtle
Embroider'd all with leaves of myrtle.

A gown made of the finest wool,
Which from our pretty lambs we pull,
Fair linèd slippers for the cold,
With buckles of the purest gold.

A belt of straw and ivy buds
With coral clasps and amber studs:
And if these pleasures may thee move,
Come live with me and be my Love.

Thy silver dishes for thy meat
As precious as the gods do eat,
Shall on an ivory table be
Prepared each day for thee and me.

The shepherd swains shall dance and sing
For thy delight each May-morning:
If these delights thy mind may move,
Then live with me and be my Love.

78

W.B. YEATS 1865-1939

THE SONG OF WANDERING AENGUS

I went out to the hazel wood,
Because a fire was in my head,
And cut and peeled a hazel wand,
And hooked a berry to a thread;
And when white moths were on the wing,
And moth-like stars were flickering out,
I dropped the berry in a stream
And caught a little silver trout.

When I had laid it on the floor
I went to blow the fire aflame,
But something rustled on the floor,
And some one called me by my name:
It had become a glimmering girl
With apple blossom in her hair
Who called me by my name and ran
And faded through the brightening air.

Though I am old with wandering
Through hollow lands and hilly lands,
I will find out where she has gone,
And kiss her lips and take her hands;
And walk among long dappled grass,
And pluck till time and times are done
The silver apples of the moon,
The golden apples of the sun.

GEORGE GORDON, LORD BYRON 1788–1824

SHE WALKS IN BEAUTY

She walks in beauty, like the night
    Of cloudless climes and starry skies;
And all that's best of dark and bright
    Meet in her aspect and her eyes:
Thus mellow'd to that tender light
    Which heaven to gaudy day denies.

One shade the more, one ray the less,
    Had half impair'd the nameless grace
Which waves in every raven tress,
    Or softly lightens o'er her face;
Where thoughts serenely sweet express
    How pure, how dear their dwelling-place.

And on that cheek, and o'er that brow,
    So soft, so calm, yet eloquent,
The smiles that win, the tints that glow,
    But tell of days in goodness spent,
A mind at peace with all below,
    A heart whose love is innocent!

A.E. HOUSMAN 1859–1936

LOVELIEST OF TREES, THE CHERRY NOW

Loveliest of trees, the cherry now
Is hung with bloom along the bough,
And stands about the woodland ride
Wearing white for Eastertide.

Now, of my threescore years and ten,
Twenty will not come again,
And take from seventy springs a score,
It only leaves me fifty more.

And since to look at things in bloom
Fifty springs are little room,
About the woodlands I will go
To see the cherry hung with snow.

JOHN DONNE 1572–1631

THE FLEA

Marke but this flea, and marke in this,
How little that which thou deny'st me is;
Mee it suck'd first, and now sucks thee,
And in this flea, our two bloods mingled bee;
Confesse it, this cannot be said
A sinne, or shame, or losse of maidenhead,
  Yet this enjoyes before it wooe,
   And pamper'd swells with one blood made of two,
   And this, alas, is more than wee would doe.

Oh stay, three lives in one flea spare,
Where wee almost, nay more than maryed are:
This flea is you and I, and this
Our marriage bed, and marriage temple is;
Though parents grudge, and you, w'are met,
And cloysterd in these living walls of Jet.
  Though use make thee apt to kill mee,
   Let not to this, selfe murder added bee,
   And sacrilege, three sinnes in killing three.

Cruell and sodaine, hast thou since
Purpled thy naile, in blood of innocence?
In what could this flea guilty bee,
Except in that drop which it suckt from thee?
Yet thou triumph'st, and saist that thou
Find'st not thy selfe, nor mee the weaker now;
  'Tis true, then learne how false, feares bee;
   Just so much honor, when thou yeeld'st to mee,
   Will wast, as this flea's death tooke life from thee.

F.W. HARVEY 1888–1957
***

DUCKS

(To F.M., Who drew them in Holzminden Prison)

I

From troubles of the world
I turn to ducks,
Beautiful comical things
Sleeping or curled
Their heads beneath white wings
By water cool,
Or finding curious things
To eat in various mucks
Beneath the pool,
Tails uppermost, or waddling
Sailor-like on the shores
Of ponds, or paddling
– Left! Right! – with fanlike feet
Which are for steady oars
When they (white galleys) float
Each bird a boat
Rippling at will the sweet
Wide waterway ...
When night is fallen *you* creep
Upstairs, but drakes and dillies
Nest with pale water-stars,
Moonbeams and shadow bars,
And water-lilies:
Fearful too much to sleep
Since they've no locks
To click against the teeth
Of weasel and fox.
And warm beneath
Are eggs of cloudy green
Whence hungry rats and lean
Would stealthily suck

New life, but for the mien
The bold ferocious mien
Of the mother-duck.

II

Yes, ducks are valiant things
On nests of twigs and straws,
And ducks are soothy things
And lovely on the lake
When that the sunlight draws
Thereon their pictures dim
In colours cool.
And when beneath the pool
They dabble, and when they swim
And make their rippling rings,
O ducks are beautiful things!
But ducks are comical things:-
As comical as you.
Quack!
They waddle round, they do.
They eat all sorts of things,
And then they quack.
By barn and stable and stack
They wander at their will,
But if you go too near
They look at you through black
Small topaz-tinted eyes
And wish you ill.
Triangular and clear
They leave their curious track
In mud at the water's edge,
And there amid the sedge
And slime they gobble and peer
Saying 'Quack! quack!'

III

When God had finished the stars and whirl of coloured suns
He turned His mind from big things to fashion little ones;
Beautiful tiny things (like daisies) He made, and then
He made the comical ones in case the minds of men
        Should stiffen and become
        Dull, humourless and glum,
And so forgetful of their Maker be
As to take even themselves – *quite seriously.*

Caterpillars and cats are lively and excellent puns:
All God's jokes are good – even the practical ones!
And as for the duck, I think God must have smiled a bit
Seeing those bright eyes blink on the day He fashioned it.
And he's probably laughing still at the sound that came out of its bill!

83

PHILIP LARKIN 1922–80

AN ARUNDEL TOMB

Side by side, their faces blurred,
The earl and countess lie in stone,
Their proper habits vaguely shown
As jointed armour, stiffened pleat,
And that faint hint of the absurd –
The little dogs under their feet.

Such plainness of the pre-baroque
Hardly involves the eye, until
It meets his left-hand gauntlet, still
Clasped empty in the other; and
One sees, with a sharp tender shock,
His hand withdrawn, holding her hand.

They would not think to lie so long.
Such faithfulness in effigy
Was just a detail friends would see:
A sculptor's sweet commissioned grace
Thrown off in helping to prolong
The Latin names around the base.

They would not guess how early in
Their supine stationary voyage
The air would change to soundless damage,
Turn the old tenantry away;
How soon succeeding eyes begin
To look, not read. Rigidly they

Persisted, linked, through lengths and breadths
Of time. Snow fell, undated. Light
Each summer thronged the glass. A bright
Litter of birdcalls strewed the same
Bone-riddled ground. And up the paths
The endless altered people came,

Washing at their identity.
Now, helpless in the hollow of
An unarmorial age, a trough
Of smoke in slow suspended skeins
Above their scrap of history,
Only an attitude remains:

Time has transfigured them into
Untruth. The stone fidelity
They hardly meant has come to be
Their final blazon, and to prove
Our almost-instinct almost true:
What will survive of us is love.

84

WILLIAM SHAKESPEARE 1564–1616

SONNET 116

Let me not to the marriage of true minds
Admit impediments. Love is not love
Which alters when it alteration finds,
Or bends with the remover to remove:
O, no, it is an ever-fixed mark,
That looks on tempests and is never shaken;
It is the star to every wandering bark,
Whose worth's unknown, although his height be taken.
Love's not Time's fool, though rosy lips and cheeks
Within his bending sickle's compass come;
Love alters not with his brief hours and weeks,
But bears it out even to the edge of doom.
    If this be error and upon me proved,
    I never writ, nor no man ever loved.

ALFRED, LORD TENNYSON 1809–92

ULYSSES

It little profits that an idle king,
By this still hearth, among these barren crags,
Match'd with an aged wife, I mete and dole
Unequal laws unto a savage race,
That hoard, and sleep, and feed, and know not me
I cannot rest from travel: I will drink
Life to the lees: all times I have enjoy'd
Greatly, have suffer'd greatly, both with those
That loved me, and alone; on shore, and when
Thro' scudding drifts the rainy Hyades
Vext the dim sea: I am become a name;
For always roaming with a hungry heart
Much have I seen and known; cities of men
And manners, climates, councils, governments,
Myself not least, but honour'd of them all;
And drunk delight of battle with my peers,
Far on the ringing plains of windy Troy.
I am a part of all that I have met;
Yet all experience is an arch wherethro'
Gleams that untravell'd world, whose margin fades
For ever and for ever when I move.
How dull it is to pause, to make an end,
To rust unburnish'd, not to shine in use!
As tho' to breathe were life. Life piled on life
Were all too little, and of one to me
Little remains: but every hour is saved
From that eternal silence, something more,
A bringer of new things; and vile it were
For some three suns to store and hoard myself,
And this grey spirit yearning in desire
To follow knowledge, like a sinking star,
Beyond the utmost bound of human thought.
      This is my son, mine own Telemachus,
To whom I leave the sceptre and the isle –
Well-loved of me, discerning to fulfil

This labour, by slow prudence to make mild
A rugged people, and thro' soft degrees
Subdue them to the useful and the good.
Most blameless is he, centred in the sphere
Of common duties, decent not to fail
In offices of tenderness, and pay
Meet adoration to my household gods,
When I am gone. He works his work, I mine.
　There lies the port: the vessel puffs her sail:
There gloom the dark broad seas. My mariners,
Souls that have toil'd, and wrought, and thought with
　　me –
That ever with a frolic welcome took
The thunder and the sunshine, and opposed
Free hearts, free foreheads – you and I are old;
Old age hath yet his honour and his toil;
Death closes all: but something ere the end,
Some work of noble note, may yet be done,
Not unbecoming men that strove with Gods.
The lights begin to twinkle from the rocks:
The long day wanes: the slow moon climbs: the deep
Moans round with many voices. Come, my friends,
'Tis not too late to seek a newer world
Push off, and sitting well in order smite
The sounding furrows; for my purpose holds
To sail beyond the sunset, and the baths
Of all the western stars, until I die.
It may be that the gulfs will wash us down:
It may be we shall touch the Happy Isles,
And see the great Achilles, whom we knew.
Tho' much is taken, much abides; and tho'
We are not now that strength which in old days
Moved earth and heaven; that which we are, we are;
One equal temper of heroic hearts,
Made weak by time and fate, but strong in will
To strive, to seek, to find, and not to yield.

LOUIS MACNEICE 1907–63

SNOW

The room was suddenly rich and the great bay-window was
Spawning snow and pink roses against it
Soundlessly collateral and incompatible:
World is suddener than we fancy it.

World is crazier and more of it than we think,
Incorrigibly plural. I peel and portion
A tangerine and spit the pips and feel
The drunkenness of things being various.

And the fire flames with a bubbling sound for world
Is more spiteful and gay than one supposes –
On the tongue on the eyes on the ears in the palms of one's hands –
There is more than glass between the snow and the huge roses

January, 1935

ROGER MCGOUGH 1937–

LET ME DIE A YOUNGMAN'S DEATH

Let me die a youngman's death
not a clean and inbetween
the sheets holywater death
not a famous-last-words
peaceful out of breath death

When I'm 73
and in constant good tumour
may I be mown down at dawn
by a bright red sports car
on my way home
from an allnight party

Or when I'm 91
with silver hair
and sitting in a barber's chair
may rival gangsters
with hamfisted tommyguns burst in
and give me a short back and insides

Or when I'm 104
and banned from the Cavern
may my mistress
catching me in bed with her daughter
and fearing for her son
cut me up into little pieces
and throw away every piece but one

Let me die a youngman's death
not a free from sin tiptoe in
candle wax and waning death
not a curtains drawn by angels borne
'what a nice way to go' death

THOMAS HARDY 1840–1928

THE RUINED MAID

'O 'Melia, my dear, this does everything crown!
Who could have supposed I should meet you in Town?
And whence such fair garments, such prosperi-ty?' –
'O didn't you know I'd been ruined,' said she.

– 'You left us in tatters, without shoes or socks,
Tired of digging potatoes, and spudding up docks;
And now you've gay bracelets and bright feathers three!' –
'Yes: that's how we dress when we're ruined,' said she.

– 'At home in the barton you said "thee" and "thou",
And "thik oon", and "theäs oon", and "t'other"; but now
Your talking quite fits 'ee for high compa-ny!'
'Some polish is gained with one's ruin,' said she.

– 'Your hands were like paws then, your face blue and bleak
But now I'm bewitched by your delicate cheek,
And your little gloves fit as on any la-dy!' –
'We never do work when we're ruined,' said she.

– 'You used to call home-life a hag-ridden dream,
And you'd sigh, and you'd sock; but at present you seem
To know not of megrims or melancho-ly' –
'True. One's pretty lively when ruined,' said she.

–'I wish I had feathers, a fine sweeping gown,
And a delicate face, and could strut about Town!' –
'My dear – a raw country girl, such as you be,
Cannot quite expect that. You ain't ruined,' said she.

Westbourne Park Villas, 1866

HUGO WILLIAMS 1942–

TOILET

I wonder will I speak to the girl
sitting opposite me on this train.
I wonder will my mouth open and say,
'Are you going all the way
to Newcastle?' or 'Can I get you a coffee?'
Or will it simply go 'aaaaah'
as if it had a mind of its own?

Half closing eggshell blue eyes,
she runs her hand through her hair
so that it clings to the carriage cloth,
then slowly frees itself.
She finds a brush and her long fair hair
flies back and forth like an African fly-whisk,
making me feel dizzy.

Suddenly, without warning,
she packs it all away in a rubber band
because I have forgotten to look out
the window for a moment.
A coffee is granted permission
to pass between her lips
and does so eagerly, without fuss.

A tunnel finds us looking out the window
into one another's eyes. She leaves her seat,
but I know that she likes me
because the light saying 'TOILET'
has come on, a sign that she is lifting
her skirt, taking down her pants
and peeing all over my face.

WILFRED OWEN 1893-1918

FUTILITY

Move him into the sun –
Gently its touch awoke him once,
At home, whispering of fields unsown.
Always it woke him, even in France,
Until this morning and this snow.
If anything might rouse him now
The kind old sun will know.

Think how it wakes the seeds, –
Woke, once, the clays of a cold star.
Are limbs, so dear-achieved, are sides,
Full-nerved – still warm – too hard to stir?
Was it for this the clay grew tall?
– O what made fatuous sunbeams toil
To break earth's sleep at all?

EDGAR ALLAN POE 1809–49

THE RAVEN

Once upon a midnight dreary, while I pondered, weak and
    weary,
Over many a quaint and curious volume of forgotten lore –
While I nodded, nearly napping, suddenly there came a
    tapping,
As of some one gently rapping – rapping at my chamber
    door
''Tis some visitor,' I muttered, 'tapping at my chamber door –
    Only this and nothing more.'

Ah, distinctly I remember, it was in the bleak December,
And each separate dying ember wrought its ghost upon the
    floor.
Eagerly I wished the morrow; – vainly I had sought to
    borrow
From my books surcease of sorrow – sorrow for the lost
    Lenore –
For the rare and radiant maiden whom the angels name
Lenore –
    Nameless here for evermore.

And the silken sad uncertain rustling of each purple curtain
Thrilled me – filled me with fantastic terrors never felt before;
So that now, to still the beating of my heart, I stood repeating
''Tis some visitor entreating entrance at my chamber door –
Some late visitor entreating entrance at my chamber door; –
    This it is and nothing more.'

Presently my soul grew stronger; hesitating then no longer,
'Sir,' said I, 'or, Madam, truly your forgiveness I implore;
But the fact is I was napping, and so gently you came rapping,
And so faintly you came tapping – tapping at my chamber
    door,
That I scarce was sure I heard you' – here I opened wide the
    door: –
    Darkness there and nothing more.

Deep into that darkness peering, long I stood there
    wondering, fearing,
Doubting, dreaming dreams no mortal ever dared to dream
    before;
But the silence was unbroken, and the darkness gave no
    token,
And the only word there spoken was the whispered word,
    'Lenore!' –
This I whispered, and an echo murmured back the word,
    'Lenore!'
        Merely this and nothing more.

Then into the chamber turning, all my soul within me
    burning.
Soon again I heard a tapping somewhat louder than before.
'Surely,' said I, 'surely that is something at my window
    lattice;
Let me see, then, what thereat is, and this mystery explore –
Let my heart be still a moment, and this mystery explore; –
        'Tis the wind and nothing more.'

Open here I flung the shutter, when, with many a flirt and
    flutter,
In there stepped a stately Raven of the saintly days of yore.
Not the least obeisance made he; not an instant stopped or
    stayed he;
But, with mien of lord or lady, perched above my chamber
    door –
Perched upon a bust of Pallas just above my chamber door –
        Perched, and sat, and nothing more.

Then this ebony bird beguiling my sad fancy into smiling,
By the grave and stern decorum of the countenance it wore,
'Though thy crest be shorn and shaven, thou,' I said, 'art
    sure no craven,
Ghastly grim and ancient Raven wandering from the

Nightly shore –
Tell me what thy Lordly name is on the Night's Plutonian
    shore!'
            Quoth the Raven, 'Nevermore.'

Much I marvelled this ungainly fowl to hear discourse so
    plainly,
Though its answer little meaning – little relevancy bore;
For we cannot help agreeing that no living human being
Ever yet was blessed with seeing bird above his chamber
    door,
Ever yet was blessed with seeing bird above his chamber
    door –
        With such name as 'Nevermore.'

But the Raven, sitting lonely on that placid bust, spoke only
That one word, as if his soul in that one word he did out-
    pour.
Nothing further then he uttered; not a feather then he
    fluttered –
Till I scarcely more than muttered, 'Other friends have
    flown before –
On the morrow *he* will leave me, as my Hopes have flown
    before.'
        Then the bird said, 'Nevermore.'

Startled at the stillness broken by reply so aptly spoken,
'Doubtless,' said I, 'what it utters is its only stock and store,
Caught from some unhappy master, whom unmerciful
    Disaster
Followed fast and followed faster till his songs one burden
    bore –
Till the dirges of his Hope the melancholy burden bore
        Of 'Never – nevermore.'

But the Raven still beguiling all my sad soul into smiling,
Straight I wheeled a cushioned seat in front of bird and bust

and door;
Then, upon the velvet sinking, I betook myself to linking
Fancy unto fancy, thinking what this ominous bird of
    yore –
What this grim, ungainly, ghastly, gaunt, and ominous
    bird of yore
        Meant in croaking 'Nevermore.'

This I sat engaged in guessing, but no syllable expressing
To the fowl whose fiery eyes now burned into my
    bosom's core;
This and more I sat divining, with my head at ease
    reclining
On the cushion's velvet violet lining that the lamp-light
    gloated o'er,
But whose velvet violet lining with the lamp-light
    gloating o'er,
        She shall press, ah, nevermore!

Then, methought, the air grew denser, perfumed from an
    unseen censer
Swung by Seraphim whose foot-falls tinkled on the
    tufted floor.
'Wretch,' I cried, 'thy God hath lent thee – by these
    angels he hath sent thee
Respite – respite and nepenthe from thy memories of
    Lenore!
Quaff, oh quaff this kind nepenthe, and forget this lost
    Lenore!'
        Quoth the Raven, 'Nevermore.'

'Prophet!' said I, 'thing of evil! – prophet still, if bird or
    devil!–
Whether Tempter sent or whether tempest tossed thee
    here ashore,

Desolate yet all undaunted, on this desert land
    enchanted –
On this home by Horror haunted – tell me truly, I implore –
Is there – *is* there balm in Gilead? – tell me – tell me, I implore!'
    Quoth the Raven, 'Nevermore.'

'Prophet!' said I, 'thing of evil – prophet still, if bird or devil!
By that Heaven that bends above us – by that God we both adore –
Tell this soul with sorrow laden if, within the distant Aidenn,
It shall clasp a sainted maiden whom the angels name Lenore –
Clasp a rare and radiant maiden whom the angels name Lenore.'
    Quoth the Raven, 'Nevermore.'

'Be that word our sign of parting, bird or fiend!' I shrieked,
    upstarting –
'Get thee back into the tempest and the Night's Plutonian shore!
Leave no black plume as a token of that lie thy soul hath spoken!
Leave my loneliness unbroken! – quit the bust above my door!
Take thy beak from out my heart, and take thy form from off my
    door!'
    Quoth the Raven, 'Nevermore.'

And the Raven, never flitting, still is sitting – still is sitting
On the pallid bust of Pallas just above my chamber door;
And his eyes have all the seeming of a Demon's that is dreaming,
And the lamp-light o'er him streaming throws his shadow on the
    floor;
And my soul from out that shadow that lies floating on the floor
    Shall be lifted – nevermore!

ROBERT BURNS 1759–96

TAM O' SHANTER

When chapman billies leave the street,
And drouthy neebors neebors meet;
As market-days are wearing late,
An' folk begin to tak the gate;
While we sit bousing at the nappy,
An' getting fou and unco happy,
We think na on the lang Scots miles,
The mosses, waters, slaps, and styles,
That lie between us and our hame,
Whare sits our sulky, sullen dame,
Gathering her brows like gathering storm,
Nursing her wrath to keep it warm.

This truth fand honest Tam o' Shanter,
As he frae Ayr ae night did canter:
(Auld Ayr, wham ne'er a town surpasses,
For honest men and bonie lasses.)

O Tam, had'st thou but been sae wise,
As taen thy ain wife Kate's advice!
She tauld thee weel thou was a skellum,
A blethering, blustering, drunken blellum;
That frae November till October,
Ae market-day thou was nae sober;
That ilka melder wi' the miller,
Thou sat as lang as thou had siller;
That ev'ry naig was ca'd a shoe on,
The smith and thee gat roaring fou on;
That at the Lord's house, even on Sunday,
Thou drank wi' Kirkton Jean till Monday.
She prophesied, that, late or soon,
Thou would be found deep drown'd in Doon,
Or catch'd wi' warlocks in the mirk
By Alloway's auld, haunted kirk.

Ah! gentle dames, it gars me greet,
To think how monie counsels sweet,
How monie lengthen'd, sage advices
The husband frae the wife despises!

But to our tale: Ae market-night,
Tam had got planted unco right,
Fast by an ingle, bleezing finely,
Wi' reaming swats, that drank divinely;
And at his elbow, Souter Johnie,
His ancient, trusty, drouthy cronie:
Tam lo'ed him like a very brither;
They had been fou for weeks thegither.
The night drave on wi' sangs and clatter;
Any ay the ale was growing better:
The landlady and Tam grew gracious
Wi' secret favours, sweet and precious:
The Souter tauld his queerest stories;
The landlord's laugh was ready chorus:
The storm without might rair and rustle,
Tam did na mind the storm a whistle.

Care, made to see a man sae happy,
E'en drown'd himself amang the nappy.
As bees flee hame wi' lades o' treasure,
The minutes wing'd their way wi' pleasure:
Kings may be blest but Tam was glorious,
O'er a' the ills o' life victorious!

But pleasures are like poppies spread:
You seize the flow'r, its bloom is shed;
Or like the snow falls in the river,
A moment white – then melts for ever;
Or like the Borealis race,
That flit ere you can point their place;
Or like the rainbow's lovely form

Evanishing amid the storm.
Nae man can tether time or tide;
The hour approaches Tam maun ride:
That hour, o' night's black arch the key-stane,
That dreary hour Tam mounts his beast in;
And sic a night he takes the road in,
As ne'er poor sinner was abroad in.

The wind blew as 'twad blawn its last;
The rattling showers rose on the blast;
The speedy gleams the darkness swallow'd;
Loud, deep and lang the thunder bellow'd:
That night, a child might understand,
The Devil had business on his hand.

Weel mounted on his gray mare Meg,
A better never lifted leg,
Tam skelpit on thro' dub and mire,
Despising wind, and rain, and fire;
Whiles holding fast his guid blue bonnet,
Whiles crooning o'er some auld Scots sonnet,
Whiles glow'ring round wi' prudent cares,
Lest bogles catch him unawares:
Kirk-Alloway was drawing nigh,
Whare ghaists and houlets nightly cry.

By this time he was cross the ford,
Whare in the snaw the chapman smoor'd;
And past the birks and meikle stane,
Whare drunken Charlie brak's neck-bane;
And thro' the whins, and by the cairn,
Whare hunters fand the murder'd bairn;
And near the thorn, aboon the well,
Whare Mungo's mither hang'd hersel.
Before him Doon pours all his floods;
The doubling storm roars thro' the woods;

The lightnings flash from pole to pole;
Near and more near the thunders roll:
When, glimmering thro' the groaning trees,
Kirk-Alloway seemed in a bleeze,
Thro' ilka bore the beams were glancing,
And loud resounded mirth and dancing.

Inspiring, bold John Barleycorn!
What dangers thou canst make us scorn!
Wi' tippenny, we fear nae evil;
Wi' usquabae, we'll face the Devil!
The swats sae ream'd in Tammie's noddle,
Fair play, he car'd na deils a boddle.
But Maggie stood, right sair astonish'd,
Till, by the heel and hand admonish'd,
She ventur'd forward on the light;
And, wow! Tam saw an unco sight!

Warlocks and witches in a dance:
Nae cotillion, brent new frae France,
But hornpipes, jigs, strathspeys, and reels,
Put life and mettle in their heels.
A winnock-bunker in the east,
There sat Auld Nick, in shape o' beast;
A tousie tyke, black, grim, and large,
To gie them music was his charge:
He screw'd the pipes and gart them skirl,
Till roof and rafters a' did dirl.
Coffins stood round, like open presses,
That shaw'd the dead in their last dresses;
And, by some devilish cantraip sleight,
Each in its cauld hand held a light:
By which heroic Tam was able
To note upon the haly table,
A murderer's banes, in gibbet-airns;
Twa span-lang, wee, unchristen'd bairns;

A thief new-cutted frae a rape –
Wi' his last gasp his gab did gape;
Five tomahawks wi' bluid red-rusted;
Five scymitars wi' murder crusted;
A garter which a babe had strangled;
A knife a father's throat had mangled –
Whom his ain so o' life bereft –
The grey hairs yet stack to the heft;
Wi' mair of horrible and awefu',
Which even to name wad be unlawfu'.

As Tammie glowr'd, amaz'd, and curious,
The mirth and fun grew fast and furious;
The piper loud and louder blew,
The dancers quick and quicker flew,
They reel'd, they set, they cross'd, they cleekit,
Till ilka carlin swat and reekit,
And coost her duddies to the wark,
And linket at it in her sark!

Now Tam, O Tam, had thae been queans,
A' plump and strapping in their teens!
Their sarks, instead o' creeshie flannen,
Been snaw-white seventeen hunder linen!
Thir breeks o' mine, my only pair,
That ance were plush, o' guid blue hair,
I wad hae gi'en them off my hurdies
For ae blink o' the bonie burdies.

But wither'd beldams, auld and droll,
Rigwoodie hags wad spean a foal,
Louping and flinging on a crummock,
I wonder didna turn thy stomach!

But Tam kend what was what fu' brawlie:
There was ae winsome wench and wawlie,
That night enlisted in the core,

Lang after kend on Carrick shore
(For monie a beast to dead she shot,
An' perish'd monie a bonie boat,
And shook baith meikle corn and bear,
And kept the country-side in fear.)
Her cutty sark, o' Paisley harn,
That while a lassie she had worn,
In longitude tho' sorely scanty,
It was her best, and she was vauntie.
Ah! little kend thy reverend grannie,
That sark she coft for her wee Nannie,
Wi' twa pund Scots ('twas a' her riches,)
Wad ever grac'd a dance of witches!

But here my Muse her wing maun cour,
Sic flights as far beyond her power:
To sing how Nannie lap and flang
(A souple jad she was and strang;)
And how Tam stood like ane bewitch'd,
And thought his very een enrich'd;
Even Satan glowr'd, and fidg'd fu' fain,
And hotch'd and blew wi' might and main;
Till first ae caper, syne anither,
Tam tint his reason a' thegither,
And roars out: 'Weel done, Cutty-sark!'
And in an instant all was dark;
And scarcely had he Maggie rallied,
When out the hellish legion sallied.

As beez bizz out wi' angry fyke,
When plundering herds assail their byke;
As open pussie's mortal foes,
When, pop! she starts before their nose;
As eager runs the market-crowd,
When 'Catch the thief!' resounds aloud:

So Maggie runs, the witches follow,
Wi' mony an eldritch skreech and hollow.

   Ah, Tam! Ah, Tam! thou'll get thy fairin!
In hell they'll roast thee like a herrin!
In vain thy Kate awaits thy comin!
Kate soon will be a woefu' woman!
Now, do thy speedy utmost, Meg,
And win the key-stane of the brig;
There, at them thou thy tail may toss,
A running stream they dare na cross!
But ere the key-stane she could make,
The fient a tail she had to shake:
For Nannie, far before the rest,
Hard upon noble Maggie prest,
And flew at Tam wi' furious ettle;
But little wist she Maggie's mettle!
Ae spring brought off her master hale,
But left behind her ain grey tail:
The carlin claught her by the rump,
And left poor Maggie scarce a stump.

   Now, wha this tale o' truth shall read,
Ilk man, and mother's son, take heed:
Whene'er to drink you are inclin'd,
Or cutty sarks run in your mind,
Think! ye may buy the joys oe'er dear:
Remember Tam o' Shanter's mare.

PERCY BYSSHE SHELLEY 1792–1822

LOVE'S PHILOSOPHY

The fountains mingle with the river
And the rivers with the ocean,
The winds of heaven mix for ever
With a sweet emotion;
Nothing in the world is single,
All things by a law divine
In one another's being mingle –
Why not I with thine?

See the mountain's kiss high heaven
And the waves clasp one another;
No sister-flower would be forgiven
If it disdain'd its brother:

And the sunlight clasps the earth,
And the moonbeams kiss the sea –
What are all these kissings worth,
If thou kiss not me?

H.W. LONGFELLOW 1807–82

from THE SONG OF HIAWATHA

X. HIAWATHA'S WOOING

'As unto the bow the cord is,
So unto the man is woman,
Though she bends him she obeys him,
Though she draws him, yet she follows,
Useless each without the other!'
Thus the youthful Hiawatha
Said within himself and pondered,
Much perplexed by various feelings,
Listless, longing, hoping, fearing,
Dreaming still of Minnehaha,
Of the lovely Laughing Water,
In the land of the Dacotahs.
'Wed a maiden of your people,'
Warning said the old Nokomis;
'Go not eastward, go not westward,
For a stranger, whom we know not!
Like a fire upon the hearth-stone
Is a neighbour's homely daughter,
Like the starlight or the moonlight
Is the handsomest of strangers!'
Thus dissuading spake Nokomis,
And my Hiawatha answered
Only this: 'Dear old Nokomis,
Very pleasant is the firelight,
But I like the starlight better,
Better do I like the moonlight!'
Gravely then said old Nokomis:
'Bring not here an idle maiden,
Bring not here a useless woman,
Hands unskilful, feet unwilling;
Bring a wife with nimble fingers,
Heart and hand that move together,
Feet that run on willing errands!'

Smiling, answered Hiawatha:
'In the land of the Dacotahs
Lives the Arrow-maker's daughter,
Minnehaha, Laughing Water,
Handsomest of all the women.
I will bring her to your wigwam,
She shall run upon your errands,
Be your starlight, moonlight, firelight,
Be the sunlight of my people!'
    Still dissuading said Nokomis:
'Bring not to my lodge a stranger
From the land of the Dacotahs,
Very fierce are the Dacotahs,
Often is there war between us,
There are feuds yet unforgotten,
Wounds that ache and still may open!'
    Laughing answered Hiawatha:
'For that reason, if no other,
Would I wed the fair Dacotah,
That our tribes might be united,
That old feuds might be forgotten,
And old wounds be healed for ever!'
    Thus departed Hiawatha
To the land of the Dacotahs,
To the land of handsome women;
Striding over moor and meadow,
Through interminable forests,
Through uninterrupted silence.
    With his moccasons of magic,
At each stride a mile he measured;
Yet the way seemed long before him,
And his heart outrun his footsteps;
And he journeyed without resting,
Till he heard the cataract's thunder,
Heard the falls of Minnehaha
Calling to him through the silence.
'Pleasant is the sound!' he murmured,
'Pleasant is the voice that calls me!'
    On the outskirts of the forest,
'Twixt the shadow and the sunshine,

Herds of fallow deer were feeding,
But they saw not Hiawatha;
To his bow he whispered, 'Fail not!'
To his arrow whispered, 'Swerve not!'
Sent it singing on its errand,
To the red heart of the roebuck;
Threw the deer across his shoulder,
And sped forward without pausing.

At the doorway of his wigwam
Sat the Ancient Arrow-maker,
In the land of the Dacotahs,
Making arrow-heads of jasper,
Arrow-heads of chalcedony.
At his side, in all her beauty,
Sat the lovely Minnehaha,
Sat his daughter, Laughing Water,
Plaiting mats of flags and rushes;
Of the past the old man's thoughts were,
And the maiden's of the future.

He was thinking, as he sat there,
Of the days when with such arrows
He had struck the deer and bison,
On the Muskoday, the meadow;
Shot the wild-goose, flying southward,
On the wing, the clamorous Wawa;
Thinking of the great war-parties,
How they came to buy his arrows.
Could not fight without his arrows.
Ah, no more such noble warriors
Could be found on earth as they were!
Now the men were all like women,
Only used their tongues for weapons!

She was thinking of a hunter,
From another tribe and country,
Young and tall, and very handsome,
Who, one morning, in the Spring-time,
Came to buy her father's arrows,
Sat and rested in the wigwam,
Lingered long about the doorway,
Looking back as he departed.

She had heard her father praise him,
Praise his courage and his wisdom;
Would he come again for arrows
To the Falls of Minnehaha?
On the mat her hands lay idle,
And her eyes were very dreamy.

Through their thoughts they heard a footstep,
Heard a rustling in the branches,
And with glowing cheek and forehead,
With the deer upon his shoulders,
Suddenly from out the woodlands
Hiawatha stood before them.

Straight the ancient Arrow-maker
Looked up gravely from his labour,
Laid aside the unfinished arrow,
Bade him enter at the doorway,
Saying, as he rose to meet him,
'Hiawatha, you are welcome!'

At the feet of Laughing Water
Hiawatha laid his burden,
Threw the red deer from his shoulders.
And the maiden looked up at him,
Looked up from her mat of rushes,
Said, with gentle look and accent,
'You are welcome, Hiawatha!'

Very spacious was the wigwam,
Made of deer-skin dressed and whitened,
With the gods of the Dacotahs,
Drawn and painted on its curtains,
And so tall the doorway, hardly
Hiawatha stooped to enter,
Hardly touched his eagle-feathers,
As he entered at the doorway.

Then uprose the Laughing Water,
From the ground fair Minnehaha,
Laid aside her mat unfinished,
Brought forth food and set before them,
Water brought them from the brooklet,
Gave them food in earthen vessels,
Gave them drink in bowls of bass-wood,

Listened while the guest was speaking,
Listened while her father answered,
But not once her lips she opened,
Not a single word she uttered.
    Yes, as in a dream she listened
To the words of Hiawatha.
As he talked of old Nokomis,
Who had nursed him in his childhood,
As he told of his companions,
Chibiabos, the musician,
And the very strong man, Kwasind,
And of happiness and plenty
In the land of the Ojibways,
In the pleasant land and peaceful.
    'After many years of warfare,
Many years of strife and bloodshed,
There is peace between the Ojibways
And the tribe of the Dacotahs.'
Thus continued Hiawatha,
And then added, speaking slowly,
'That this peace may last for ever,
And our hands be clasped more closely,
And our hearts be more united,
Give me as my wife this maiden,
Minnehaha, Laughing Water,
Loveliest of Dacotah women!'
    And the ancient Arrow-maker
Paused a moment ere he answered,
Smoked a little while in silence,
Looked at Hiawatha proudly,
Fondly looked at Laughing Water,
And made answer, very gravely,
'Yes, if Minnehaha wishes;
Let your heart speak, Minnehaha!'
    And the lovely Laughing Water
Seemed more lovely, as she stood there,
Neither willing nor reluctant,
As she went to Hiawatha,
Softly took the seat beside him,
While she said, and blushed to say it,

'I will follow you, my husband!'
    This was Hiawatha's wooing!
Thus it was he won the daughter
Of the ancient Arrow-maker,
In the land of the Dacotahs!

    From the wigwam he departed,
Leading with him Laughing Water,
Hand in hand they went together,
Through the woodland and the meadow
Left the old man standing lonely
At the door of his wigwam,
Heard the Falls of Minnehaha
Calling to them from the distance,
Crying to them from afar off,
'Fare thee well, O Minnehaha!'

    And the ancient Arrow-maker
Turned again unto his labour,
Sat down by his sunny doorway,
Murmuring to himself, and saying,
'Thus it is our daughters leave us,
Those we love, and those who love us.
Just when they have learned to help us.
When we are old and lean upon them,
Comes a youth with flaunting feathers,
With his flute of reeds, a stranger
Wanders piping through the village,
Beckons to the fairest maiden,
And she follows where he leads her,
Leaving all things for the stranger!'

    Pleasant was the journey homeward,
Through the interminable forests,
Over meadow, over mountain,
Over river, hill and hollow.
Short it seemed to Hiawatha,
Though they journeyed very slowly,
Though his pace he checked and slackened
To the steps of Laughing Water.

    Over wide and rushing rivers
In his arms he bore the maiden;
Light he thought her as a feather,

As the plume upon his head-gear;
Cleared the tangled pathway for her,
Bent aside the swaying branches,
Made at night a lodge of branches,
And a bed with boughs of hemlock,
And a fire before the doorway
With the dry cones of the pine-tree.

All the travelling winds went with them
O'er the meadow, through the forest;
All the stars of night looked at them,
Watched with sleepless eyes their slumber;
From his ambush in the oak-tree
Peeped the squirrel, Ajidaumo,
Watched with eager eyes the lovers.
And the rabbit, the Wabasso,
Scampered from the path before them,
Peering, peeping from his burrow,
Sat erect upon his haunches,
Watched with curious eyes the lovers.

Pleasant was the journey homeward,
All the birds sang loud and sweetly
Songs of happiness and heart's-ease;
Sang the blue-bird, the Owaissa,
'Happy are you, Hiawatha,
Having such a wife to love you!'
Sang the Opechee, the robin,
'Happy are you, Laughing Water,
Having such a noble husband!'

From the sky the sun benignant
Looked upon them through the branches,
Saying to them, 'O my children,
Love is sunshine, hate is shadow,
Life is checkered shade and sunshine;
Rule by love, O Hiawatha!'

From the sky the moon looked at them,
Filled the lodge with mystic splendours,
Whispered to them, 'O my children,
Day is restless, night is quiet,
Man imperious, woman feeble;
Half is mine, although I follow;

Rule by patience, Laughing Water!'
   Thus it was they journeyed homeward;
Thus it was that Hiawatha
To the lodge of old Nokomis
Brought the moonlight, starlight, firelight,
Brought the sunshine of his people,
Minnehaha, Laughing Water,
Handsomest of all the women
In the land of the Dacotahs,
In the land of handsome women.

GERARD MANLEY HOPKINS 1844-89

GOD'S GRANDEUR

The world is charged with the grandeur of God.
    It will flame out, like shining from shook foil;
    It gathers to a greatness, like the ooze of oil
Crushed. Why do men then now not reck his rod?
Generations have trod, have trod, have trod;
    And all is seared with trade; bleared, smeared with toil;
    And wears man's smudge and shares man's smell: the soil
Is bare now, nor can foot feel, being shod.

And for all this, nature is never spent;
    There lives the dearest freshness deep down things;
And though the last lights off the black West went
    Oh, morning, at the brown brink eastward, springs –
Because the Holy Ghost over the bent
    World broods with warm breast and with ah! bright wings.

MICHAEL ROSEN 1954–

CHOCOLATE CAKE

I love chocolate cake.
And when I was a boy
I loved it even more.

Sometimes we used to have it for tea
and Mum used to say,
'If there's any left over
you can have it to take to school
tomorrow to have at playtime.'
And the next day I would take it to school
wrapped up in tin foil
open it up at playtime and sit in the
corner of the playground
eating it,
you know how the icing on top
is all shiny and it cracks as you
bite into it,
and there's that other kind of icing in
the middle
and it sticks to your hands and you
can lick your fingers
and lick your lips
oh it's lovely.
yeah.

Anyway,
once we had this chocolate cake for tea
and later I went to bed
but while I was in bed
I found myself waking up
licking my lips
and smiling.
I woke up proper.
'The chocolate cake.'
It was the first thing
I thought of.

I could almost see it
so I thought,
what if I go downstairs
and have a little nibble, yeah?

It was all dark
everyone was in bed
so it must have been really late
but I got out of bed,
crept out of the door

there's always a creaky floorboard, isn't there?

Past Mum and Dad's room,

careful not to tread on bits of broken toys
or bits of Lego
you know what it's like treading on Lego
with your bare feet,

yowwww
shhhhhhh

downstairs
into the kitchen
open the cupboard
and there it is
all shining.

So I take it out of the cupboard
put it on the table
and I see that
there's a few crumbs lying about on the plate,
so I lick my finger and run my finger all over the crumbs
scooping them up
and put them into my mouth.

ooooooooommmmmmmmmm

nice.

Then
I look again
and on one side where it's been cut,
it's all crumbly.

So I take a knife
I think I'll just tidy that up a bit,
cut off the crumbly bits
scoop them all up
and into the mouth

oooooommm mmmm
nice.

Look at the cake again.

That looks a bit funny now,
one side doesn't match the other
I'll just even it up a bit, eh?

Take the knife
and slice.
This time the knife makes a little cracky noise
as it goes through that hard icing on top.

A whole slice this time,

into the mouth.

Oh the icing on top
and the icing in the middle
ohhhhhh oooo mmmmmm.

But now
I can't stop myself
Knife –
I just take any old slice at it
and I've got this great big chunk
and I'm cramming it in
what a greedy pig
but it's so nice,

and there's another
and another and I'm squealing and I'm smacking my lips
and I'm stuffing myself with it
and
before I know
I've eaten the lot.
The whole lot.

I look at the plate.
It's all gone.

Oh no
they're bound to notice, aren't they,
a whole chocolate cake doesn't just disappear
does it?

What shall I do?

I know. I'll wash the plate up,
and the knife

and put them away and maybe no one
will notice, eh?

So I do that
and creep creep creep
back to bed
into bed
doze off
licking my lips
with a lovely feeling in my belly.
Mmmmmmmmmm.

In the morning I get up,
downstairs,
have breakfast,
Mum's saying,
'Have you got your dinner money?'
and I say,
'Yes.'
'And don't forget to take some chocolate cake with you.'
I stopped breathing.

'What's the matter,' she says,
'you normally jump at chocolate cake?'

I'm still not breathing,
and she's looking at me very closely now.

She's looking at me just below my mouth.
'What's that?' she says.
'What's what?' I say.

'What's that there?'
'Where?'
'There,' she says, pointing at my chin.
'I don't know,' I say.
'It looks like chocolate,' she says.
'It's not chocolate is it?'
No answer.
'Is it?'
'I don't know.'
She goes to the cupboard
looks in, up, top, middle, bottom,
turns back to me.
'It's gone.
It's gone.
You haven't eaten it, have you?'
'I don't know.'
'You don't know. You don't know if you've eaten a whole
chocolate cake or not?
When? When did you eat it?'

So I told her,

and she said
well what could she say?
'That's the last time I give you any cake to take
to school.
Now go. Get out
no wait
not before you've washed your dirty sticky face.'
I went upstairs
looked in the mirror
and there it was,
just below my mouth,
a chocolate smudge.
The give-away.
Maybe she'll forget about it by next week.

LEIGH HUNT 1784–1859

JENNY KISSED ME

Jenny kiss'd me when we met,
　Jumping from the chair she sat in;
Time, you thief, who love to get
　Sweets into your list, put that in!
Say I'm weary, say I'm sad,
　Say that health and wealth have miss'd me,
Say I'm growing old, but add,
　Jenny kiss'd me.

SEAMUS HEANEY 1939–

BLACKBERRY-PICKING

FOR PHILIP HOBSBAUM

Late august, given heavy rain and sun
For a full week, the blackberries would ripen.
At first, just one, a glossy purple clot
Among others, red, green, hard as a knot.
You ate that first one and its flesh was sweet
Like thickened wine: summer's blood was in it
Leaving stains upon the tongue and lust for
Picking. Then red ones inked up and that hunger
Sent us out with milk-cans, pea-tins, jam-pots
Where briars scratched and wet grass bleached our
    boots.
Round hayfields, cornfields and potato-drills
We trekked and picked until the cans were full,
Until the tinkling bottom had been covered
With green ones, and on top big dark blobs burned
Like a plate of eyes. Our hands were peppered
With thorn pricks, our palms sticky as Bluebeard's.

We hoarded the fresh berries in the byre.
But when the bath was filled we found a fur,
A rat-grey fungus, glutting on our cache.
The juice was stinking too. Once off the bush
The fruit fermented, the sweet flesh would turn sour.
I always felt like crying. It wasn't fair
That all the lovely canfuls smelt of rot.
Each year I hoped they'd keep, knew they would not.

WILLIAM WORDSWORTH 1770–1850

from THE PRELUDE

CHILDHOOD AND SCHOOL-TIME

Fair seed-time had my soul, and I grew up
Foster'd alike by beauty and by fear;
Much favour'd in my birthplace, and no less
In that beloved Vale to which, erelong,
I was transplanted. Well I call to mind
('Twas at an early age, ere I had seen
Nine summers) when upon the mountain slope
The frost and breath of frosty wind had snapp'd
The last autumnal crocus, 'twas my joy
To wander half the night among the Cliffs
And the smooth Hollows, where the woodcocks ran
Along the open turf. In thought and wish
That time, my shoulder all with springes hung,
I was a fell destroyer. On the heights
Scudding away from snare to snare, I plied
My anxious visitation, hurrying on,
Still hurrying, hurrying onward; moon and stars
Were shining o'er my head; I was alone,
and seem'd to be a trouble to the peace
That was among them. Sometimes it befel
In these night-wanderings, that a strong desire
O'erpower'd my better reason, and the bird
Which was the captive of another's toils
Became my prey; and, when the deed was done
I heard among the solitary hills
Low breathings coming after me, and sounds
Of undistinguishable motion, steps
Almost as silent as the turf they trod.
Nor less in springtime when on southern banks
The shining sun had from his knot of leaves
Decoy'd the primrose flower, and when the Vales
And woods were warm, was I a plunderer then
In the high places, on the lonesome peaks

Where'er, among the mountains and the winds,
The Mother Bird had built her lodge. Though mean
My object, and inglorious, yet the end
Was not ignoble. Oh! when I have hung
Above the raven's nest, by knots of grass
And half-inch fissures in the slippery rock
But ill sustain'd, and almost, as it seem'd,
Suspended by the blast which blew amain,
Shouldering the naked crag; Oh! at that time,
While on the perilous ridge I hung alone,
With what strange utterance did the loud dry wind
Blow through my ears! the sky seem'd not a sky
Of earth, and with what motion mov'd the clouds!

* * * * * * *

The moon was up, the Lake was shining clear
Among the hoary mountains; from the Shore
I push'd, and struck the oars and struck again
In cadence, and my little Boat mov'd on
Even like a Man who walks with stately step
Though bent on speed. It was an act of stealth
And troubled pleasure; not without the voice
Of mountain-echoes did my Boat move on,
Leaving behind her still on either side
Small circles glittering idly in the moon,
Until they melted all into one track
Of sparkling light. A rocky Steep uprose
Above the Cavern of the Willow tree
And now, as suited one who proudly row'd
With his best skill, I fix'd a steady view
Upon the top of that same craggy ridge,
The bound of the horizon, for behind
Was nothing but the stars and the grey sky.
She was an elfin Pinnace; lustily
I dipp'd my oars into the silent Lake,

And, as I rose upon the stroke, my Boat
Went heaving through the water, like a Swan;
When from behind that craggy Steep, till then
The bound of the horizon, a huge Cliff,
As if with voluntary power instinct,
Uprear'd its head. I struck and struck again,
And, growing still in stature the huge Cliff
Rose up between me and the stars, and still,
With measur'd motion, like a living thing,
Strode after me. With trembling hands I turn'd,
And through the silent water stole my way
Back to the Cavern of the Willow tree.
There, in her morning-place, I left my Bark,
And, through the meadows homeward went, with grave
And serious thoughts; and after I had seen
That spectacle, for many days, my brain
Work'd with a dim and undetermin'd sense
Of unknown modes of being; in my thoughts
There was a darkness, call it solitude,
Or blank desertion, no familiar shapes
Of hourly objects, images of trees,
Of sea or sky, no colours of green fields;
But huge and mighty Forms that do not live
Like living men mov'd slowly through the mind
By day and were the trouble of my dreams.

Wisdom and Spirit of the Universe!
Thou Soul that art the eternity of thought!
That giv'st to forms and images a breath
And everlasting motion! not in vain,
By day or star-light thus from my first dawn
Of Childhood didst Thou intertwine for me
The passions that build up our human Soul,
Not with the mean and vulgar works of Man,
But with high objects, with enduring things,

With life and nature, purifying thus
The elements of feeling and of thought,
And sanctifying, by such discipline,
Both pain and fear, until we recognize
A grandeur in the beatings of the heart.
    Nor was this fellowship vouchsaf'd to me
With stinted kindness. In November days,
When vapours, rolling down the valleys, made
A lonely scene more lonesome; among woods
At noon, and 'mid the calm of summer nights,
When, by the margin of the trembling Lake,
Beneath the gloomy hills I homeward went
In solitude, such intercourse was mine;
'Twas mine among the fields both day and night,
And by the waters all the summer long.

    And in the frosty season, when the sun
Was set, and visible for many a mile
The cottage windows through the twilight blaz'd,
I heeded not the summons:- happy time
It was, indeed, for all of us; to me
It was a time of rapture: clear and loud
The village clock toll'd six; I wheel'd about,
Proud and exulting, like an untir'd horse,
That cares not for his home. – All shod with steel,
We hiss'd along the polish'd ice, in games
Confederate, imitative of the chace
And woodland pleasures, the resounding horn,
The Pack loud bellowing, and the hunted hare.
So through the darkness and the cold we flew,
And not a voice was idle; with the din,
Meanwhile, the precipices rang aloud,
The leafless trees, and every icy crag
Tinkled like iron, while the distant hills
Into the tumult sent an alien sound

Of melancholy, not unnoticed, while the stars,
Eastward, were sparkling clear, and in the west
The orange sky of evening died away.

Not seldom from the uproar I retired
Into a silent bay, or sportively
Glanced sideway, leaving the tumultuous throng,
To cut across the image of a star
That gleam'd upon the ice: and oftentimes
When we had given our bodies to the wind,
And all the shadowy banks, on either side,
Came sweeping through the darkness, spinning still
The rapid line of motion; then at once
Have I, reclining back upon my heels,
Stopp'd short, yet still the solitary Cliffs
Wheeled by me, even as if the earth had roll'd
With visible motion her diurnal round;
Behind me did they stretch in solemn train
Feebler and feebler, and I stood and watch'd
Till all was tranquil as a dreamless sleep.

    ['There Was A Boy']

There was a boy, ye knew him well, ye Cliffs
And Islands of Winander! many a time
At evening, when the stars had just begun
To move along the edges of the hills,
Rising or setting, would he stand alone
Beneath the trees, or by the glimmering Lake,
And there, with fingers interwoven, both hands
Press'd closely, palm to palm, and to his mouth
Uplifted, he, as through an instrument,
Blew mimic hootings to the silent owls
That they might answer him. – And they would shout
Across the watery Vale, and shout again,
Responsive to his call, with quivering peals,

And long halloos, and screams, and echoes loud
Redoubled and redoubled; concourse wild
Of mirth and jocund din! And when it chanced
That pauses of deep silence mock'd his skill,
Then sometimes, in that silence, while he hung
Listening, a gentle shock of mild surprize
Has carried far into his heart the voice
Of mountain torrents; or the visible scene
Would enter unawares into his mind
With all its solemn imagery, its rocks,
Its woods, and that uncertain Heaven, receiv'd
Into the bosom of the steady Lake.

CONCLUSION

It was a Summer's night, a close warm night,
Wan, dull and glaring, with a dripping mist
Low-hung and thick that cover'd all the sky,
Half-threatening storm and rain; but on we went
Uncheck'd, being full of heart and having faith
In our tried Pilot. Little could we see
Hemm'd round on every side with fog and damp,
And, after ordinary travellers' chat
With our Conductor, silently we sank
Each into commerce with his private thoughts:
Thus did we breast the ascent, and by myself
Was nothing either seen or heard the while
Which took me from my musings, save that once
The Shepherd's Cur did to his own great joy
Unearth a hedgehog in the mountain crags
Round which he made a barking turbulent.
This small adventure, for even such it seemed
In that wild place and at the dead of night,
Being over and forgotten, on we wound
In silence as before. With forehead bent
Earthward, as if in opposition set

Against an enemy, I panted up
With eager pace, and no less eager thoughts.
Thus might we wear perhaps an hour away,
Ascending at loose distance each from each,
And I, as chanced, the foremost of the Band;
When at my feet the ground appear'd to brighten,
And with a step or two seem'd brighter still;
Nor had I time to ask the cause of this,
For instantly a Light upon the turf
Fell like a flash: I looked about, and lo!
The Moon stood naked in the Heavens, at height
Immense above my head, and on the shore
I found myself of a huge sea of mist,
Which, meek and silent, rested at my feet:
A hundred hills their dusky backs upheaved
All over this still Ocean, and beyond,
Far, far beyond, the vapours shot themselves,
In headlands, tongues, and promontory shapes,
Into the Sea, the real Sea, that seem'd
To dwindle, and give up its majesty,
Usurp'd upon as far as sight could reach.
Meanwhile, the Moon look'd down upon this shew
In single glory, and we stood, the mist
Touching our very feet; and from the shore
At distance not the third part of a mile
Was a blue chasm; a fracture in the vapour,
A deep and gloomy breathing-place through which
Mounted the roar of waters, torrents, streams
Innumerable, roaring with one voice.
The universal spectacle throughout
Was shaped for admiration and delight,
Grand in itself alone, but in that breach
Through which the homeless voice of waters rose,
That dark deep thoroughfare had Nature lodg'd
The Soul, the Imagination of the whole.

CAROL ANN DUFFY 1955–

WARMING HER PEARLS

Next to my own skin, her pearls. My mistress
bids me wear them, warm them, until evening
when I'll brush her hair. At six, I place them
round her cool, white throat. All day I think of her,

resting in the Yellow room, contemplating silk
or taffeta, which gown tonight? She fans herself
whilst I work willingly, my slow heat entering
each pearl. Slack on my neck, her rope.

She's beautiful. I dream about her
in my attic bed; picture her dancing
with tall men, puzzled by my faint persistent scent
beneath her French perfume, her milky stones.

I dust her shoulders with a rabbit's foot,
watch the soft blush seep through her skin
like an indolent sigh. In her looking-glass
my red lips part as though I want to speak.

Full moon. Her carriage brings her home. I see
her every movement in my head ... Undressing,
taking off her jewels, her slim hand reaching
for the case, slipping naked into bed, the way

she always does ... And I lie here awake,
knowing the pearls are cooling even now
in the room where my mistress sleeps. All night
I feel their absence and I burn.

ACKNOWLEDGEMENTS

— ✧ —

The publishers would like to acknowledge the following for permission to reproduce copyright material.

1, 46, 48. A.P. Watt Ltd on behalf of The National Trust for Places of Historic Interest or Natural Beauty for 'If', 'The Glory of the Garden' and 'The Way Through the Woods' from *Rudyard Kipling's Verse: Definitive Edition*.

3,63. The Literary Trustees of Walter de la Mare and the Society of Authors as their representative for 'The Listeners' and 'Silver'.

4. James MacGibbon for 'Not Waving but Drowning' from *The Collected Poems of Stevie Smith* (Penguin Twentieth Century Classics).

7, 10, 37, 78. A.P. Watt on behalf of Michael Yeats for 'The Lake Isle of Innisfree', 'He Wishes for the Cloths of Heaven' and 'When You Are Old', and 'Song of the Wandering Aengus' from *The Collected Poems of W B Yeats*.

13, 35. J.M. Dent for 'Fern Hill' and 'Do Not Go Gentle Into That Good Night' from *The Poems* by Dylan Thomas.

14. 'Leisure' from the *Complete Poems of W.H. Davies* published by Jonathan Cape.

15. John Murray (Publishers) Ltd for 'The Highwayman' by Alfred Noyes from his *Collected Poems*.

19. Faber and Faber Ltd for 'Stop all the clocks, cut off the telephone' from 'Twelve Songs' by W.H. Auden from his *Collected Poems*.

22. 'Warning' from *Selected Poems* by Jenny Joseph, published by Bloodaxe 1992.

23, 27. The Society of Authors as the literary representative of the Estate of John Masefield for 'Sea Fever' and 'Cargoes'.

26, 44, 52, 72. Faber and Faber Ltd for 'The Love Song of J. Alfred Prufrock', 'Journey of the Magi', 'La Figlia Che Piange' and 'Preludes' from T.S. Eliot's *Collected Poems 1909-1962*.

31, 47. 'Stopping by Woods on a Snowy Evening' and 'The Road Not Taken' from *Poetry of Robert Frost* edited by Edward Connery Lathem published by Jonathan Cape.

33. 'Everyone Sang' by Siegfried Sassoon. Reprinted by permission of George Sassoon.

38. 'Naming of Parts' from Henry Reed's *Collected Poems* edited by Jon Stallworthy (1991). Reprinted by permission of Oxford University Press.

39, 67, 88. Papermac for 'The Darkling Thrush', 'Afterwards' and 'The Ruined Maid' from *The Complete Poems* by Thomas Hardy.

40. 'Please Mrs Butler' from *Please Mrs Butler* by Allan Ahlberg. Reprinted by permission of Penguin.

43. *This England* magazine for permission to reproduce 'High Flight' by John Gillespie McGee.

50. Faber and Faber Ltd for 'Bloody Men' from *Serious Concerns* by Wendy Cope.

53, 56, 83. Faber and Faber Ltd for 'The Whitsun Weddings', 'This Be The Verse' and 'An Arundel Tomb' from *Collected Poems* by Philip Larkin.

57. Laurence Pollinger Ltd and the Estate of Frieda Lawrence Ravagli for 'Snake' from *The Complete Poems of D.H. Lawrence*.

60, 65, 86. Faber and Faber Ltd for 'The Sunlight on the Garden', 'Prayer Before Birth' and 'Snow' by Louis MacNeice from his *Collected Poems*.

62, 70. John Murray (Publishers) Ltd for 'Diary of a Church Mouse' and 'Christmas' by John Betjeman from his *Collected Poems*.

66. Faber and Faber Ltd for 'Macavity: the Mystery Cat' from *Old Possum's Book of Practical Cats* by T.S. Eliot.

71. Faber and Faber Ltd for 'The Thought Fox' from *The Hawk In The Rain* by Ted Hughes.

80. The Society of Authors as the literary representative of the Estate of A.E. Housman for 'Loveliest of Trees'.

87. Peters Fraser & Dunlop Group for 'Let Me Die a Youngman's Death' from *The Mersey Sound* by Roger McGough.

89. 'Toilet' from *Self Portrait with a Slide* by Hugo Williams (1990). Reprinted by permission of Oxford University Press.

96. 'Chocolate Cake' from *Quick Let's Get Out Of Here* by Michael Rosen published by Scholastic Limited.

98. Faber and Faber Ltd for 'Blackberry-Picking' from *Death Of A Naturalist* by Seamus Heaney.

100. 'Warming Her Pearls' is taken from *Selling Manhattan* by Carol Ann Duffy, published by Anvil Press Poetry in 1987.

The Publishers have made every effort to trace copyright holders of material reproduced within this compilation. If, however, they have inadvertently made any error they would be grateful for notification.

INDEX OF POETS' NAMES

— ✧ —

INDEX OF FIRST LINES

— ⬧ —

— ✦ —

— ✧ —

— ◇ —